OUTDOOR SCHOOL

GARDENING

An imprint of Macmillan Publishing Group, LLC
120 Broadway, New York, NY 10271
OddDot.com

Odd Dot ® is a registered trademark of Macmillan Publishing Group, LLC

Outdoor School is a trademark of Odd Dot.
Text copyright © 2024 by Bridget Heos
Illustrations copyright © 2024 by John D. Dawson
Library of Congress Cataloging-in-Publication Data is available.
ISBN 978-1-250-26285-1

OUTDOOR SCHOOL LOGO DESIGNER Tae Won Yu
COVER DESIGNER Christina Quintero
INTERIOR DESIGNER Christina Quintero & Phil Conigliaro
EDITOR Julia Sooy
ILLUSTRATOR John D. Dawson
MAP DESIGNER Caitlyn Hunter

Illustration credits: Art from *Golden Guides: Birds* by James Gordon Irving; *Butterflies and Moths* by Andre Durenceau; *Trees* by Dorothea and Sy Barlowe; *Trees of North America* by Rebecca Marrilees; *Poisonous Animals* by John D. Dawson; *Weeds* by Jean Zallinger; and *Wildflowers* by Rudolf Freund.
Select images from Biodiversity Heritage Library | www.biodiversitylibrary.org
Cover images used under license from Shutterstock.com

Our books may be purchased in bulk for promotional, educational, or business use. Please contact your local bookseller or the Macmillan Corporate and Premium Sales Department at (800) 221-7945 ext. 5442 or by email at MacmillanSpecialMarkets@macmillan.com.

Printed in China by 1010 Printing International Limited, Kwun Tong, Hong Kong

First edition, 2024

1 3 5 7 9 10 8 6 4 2

OUTDOOR SCHOOL

GARDENING

BRIDGET HEOS

ILLUSTRATED BY
JOHN D. DAWSON

Odd Dot 👀 New York

CONTENTS

OUTDOOR SCHOOL

OPEN YOUR DOOR.
STEP **OUTSIDE.**
YOU'VE JUST WALKED INTO
OUTDOOR SCHOOL.

Whether you're entering an urban wilderness or a remote forest, at Outdoor School we have only four guidelines.

→ BE AN EXPLORER, A RESEARCHER, AND—MOST OF ALL—A LEADER.

→ TAKE CHANCES AND SOLVE PROBLEMS AFTER CONSIDERING ANY RISKS.

→ FORGE A RESPECTFUL RELATIONSHIP WITH NATURE AND YOURSELF.

→ BE FREE, BE WILD, AND BE BRAVE.

We believe that people learn best through doing. So we not only give you information about the wild, but we also include three kinds of activities:

TRY IT → Read about the topic and experience it right away.

TRACK IT ↘ Observe and interact with the plants, and reflect on your experiences right in this book.

TAKE IT TO THE NEXT LEVEL ↗ Progress to advanced techniques and master a skill.

Completed any of these activities? Awesome! Check off your accomplishment and write in the date.

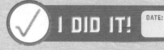

✓ **I DID IT!** DATE:

This book is the guide to the adventures you've been waiting for. We hope you'll do something outside your comfort zone—but we're not telling you to go out of your way to find danger. If something makes you uncomfortable, don't do it.

Don't forget: This book is **YOURS**, so use it. Write in it, draw in it, make notes about your favorite waterfall hike in it, dry a flower in it, whatever! The purpose of Outdoor School is to help you learn about your world, help you learn about yourself, and—best of all—help you have an epic adventure.

So now that you have everything you need—keep going. Take another step. And another. And never stop.

Yours in adventure,

THE OUTDOOR SCHOOL TEAM

PART I

ELEMENTS OF GARDENING

J. DAWSON

What would YOU do?

On a field trip to a historical house and

garden, you are given a packet of heirloom tomato seeds. The tour guide explains that heirloom seeds are seeds that have been passed on from generation to generation but were never planted on a large scale. You can plant them at home. Then when the tomatoes grow, you can preserve the seeds to use again.

You rush home after school, eager to grow your tomato garden. But staring at your backyard, you have no idea where or how to plant tomatoes. *What would you do?*

CHAPTER 1

What a Plant Needs

When people began not only foraging for plants but growing them, it changed the world. Those who adopted this lifestyle settled in permanent villages, which grew into cities and even empires. World population soared. People had less free time but more plentiful food (except in times of famine). As farming societies tended to develop different social classes, people had less equality but more luxuries (though not available to all). They had less room to roam but more tools with which to understand the universe. And it all started with some seeds.

Early farmers did not know that their lifestyle would give rise to empires. In fact, early farming was a hardscrabble way of life. Archaeologists theorize that it all started when people settled on land so rich in wild plants and animals that they were able to "stay put." In time, they saw their land as their private property. Even when wild resources dwindled, the people stayed. They survived by cultivating seeds and, later, animals. This shift, known as the Agricultural Revolution, began around twelve thousand years ago and happened separately on different continents. In time, methods became more sophisticated and society more complex. It is all rooted in a simple idea: If you plant a seed and give it the proper care, it will grow.

As such, anyone can grow a garden, but it does require time and knowledge. As early farmers learned, wild seeds travel where the wind takes them and grow where they will. But seeds that we plant require care. The first step is planning. Think about what you would like to grow. Fresh food for your family? Flowers for decoration? Plants native to your region? Also think about what you *can* grow based on your ability to meet the plants' basic needs. Every plant needs air, sunlight, the right temperature, room to grow, water, and nutrients. Air is a given,

PLAN OF THE GARDENS AT MONTAGUE HOUSE, WHITEHALL

which leaves five needs to consider when planning your garden.

In this book, you will learn some gardening basics. Then you'll read about how to grow herbs, vegetables, fruit, flowers, and other plants. Along the way, you'll develop skills that will allow you to grow your own garden. At the end, you'll come up with a plan to turn your whole yard into a garden!

Sunlight

If multiple garden locations are available, choose one that is sunny for at least six hours a day—the amount many plants need to grow. To determine the sunniest parts of your yard, picture the way the sun "moves" across the sky. The sun may rise in the east and set in the west, but its location in the sky varies throughout the year. Imagine three arches. The medium-size arch shows the path of the sun at spring and fall equinox, when the sun rises and sets at the equator—beginning at true east and ending at true west. The smallest arch shows the sun at winter solstice—the shortest day of the year. Here, the sun rises at a southeast point and sets at a southwest point. At summer solstice, the longest day of the year, the largest arch begins at a northeast point and ends at a northwest point. Now, here's the really important part. In the Northern Hemisphere, the arches all tilt toward the south!

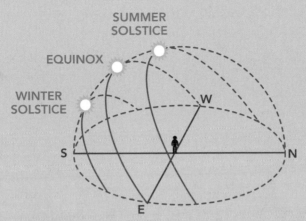

That means that for most of the day, the sun is shining down from the southern sky. Think of the structures in and around your yard. The area to the north of a tree, house, wall, or building will be shady for much of the day. On the other hand, the south side of taller objects will still be sunny. In fact, a south-facing wall or hill will collect heat throughout the day, making the area around it a little warmer than other areas. This is known as a microclimate.

Because the sun rises in the east and sets in the west, areas to the east of a tree, building, or house will receive morning sunlight and afternoon shade, whereas areas to the west will get morning shade and afternoon sun. In hot climates, morning sun and afternoon shade is best so that plants don't overheat. But if you choose plants that don't mind the heat, and give them plenty of water, afternoon sun is fine, too.

For all plants to get the same amount of sunlight, you want to plant your tallest plants on the north side of your garden. However, if you'd like to shade some cooler-weather crops so that they survive the summer, you can plant taller crops on the south side. For rectangular gardens, growers tend to orient them from north to south, believing this provides all plants with maximum sunlight.

If you have little sunlight anywhere in your yard, you'll have to settle for shade-loving plants. Or find a community garden with sunny, fertile plots available for rent.

Each plant description in this book includes a sunlight requirement. Here is what each description means:

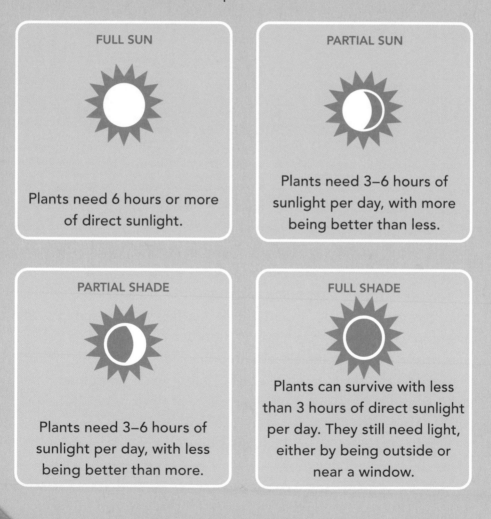

FULL SUN

Plants need 6 hours or more of direct sunlight.

PARTIAL SUN

Plants need 3–6 hours of sunlight per day, with more being better than less.

PARTIAL SHADE

Plants need 3–6 hours of sunlight per day, with less being better than more.

FULL SHADE

Plants can survive with less than 3 hours of direct sunlight per day. They still need light, either by being outside or near a window.

> ### WHAT YOU'LL NEED

> ➢ a pencil and a blanket or tarp at least the
> size of your planned garden

Mark your chosen garden location with a blanket. A garden
can be as small as a single potted plant or as large as your
entire outdoor property. For a beginner garden, typical
sizes are: three pots, ranging from small (1 gallon/4 L) to
large (15 gallons/ 56.5 L), a 4x4 foot (1x1 m) raised garden
bed, or a 4x12 foot (1x3.5 m) plot.

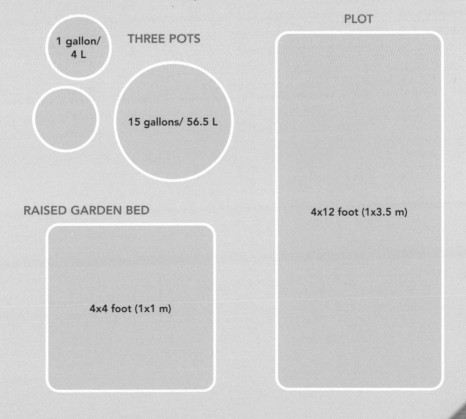

PLOT

THREE POTS

1 gallon/
4 L

15 gallons/ 56.5 L

RAISED GARDEN BED

4x12 foot (1x3.5 m)

4x4 foot (1x1 m)

From sunup to sundown, check the blanket every hour and circle whether there is sun, shade, or both. If you leave the house, ask a family member to record the sunlight.

5: 00 a.m. ☼ ☽ ☀ ☀   2: 00 p.m. ☼ ☼ ☀ ☀

6: 00 a.m. ☼ ☽ ☀ ☀   3: 00 p.m. ☼ ☼ ☀ ☀

7: 00 a.m. ☼ ☽ ☀ ☀   4: 00 p.m. ☼ ☼ ☀ ☀

8: 00 a.m. ☼ ☽ ☀ ☀   5: 00 p.m. ☼ ☽ ☀ ☀

9: 00 a.m. ☼ ☽ ☀ ☀   6: 00 p.m. ☼ ☼ ☀ ☀

10: 00 a.m. ☼ ☼ ☀ ☀   7: 00 p.m. ☼ ☼ ☀ ☀

11: 00 a.m. ☼ ☽ ☀ ☀   8: 00 p.m. ☼ ☼ ☀ ☀

12: 00 p.m. ☼ ☽ ☀ ☀   9: 00 p.m. ☼ ☽ ☀ ☀

1: 00 p.m. ☼ ☽ ☀ ☀

How many total hours of sunlight will your garden have?

Which of these categories does your garden fall into?

I DID IT! DATE:

8

The Right Temperature

Plants vary in the temperature they prefer. Some can't tolerate any cold, whereas others need to freeze over the winter to remain healthy. The USDA grow zone map designates areas based on their average minimum temperatures. Then plants can be matched to their preferred zones.

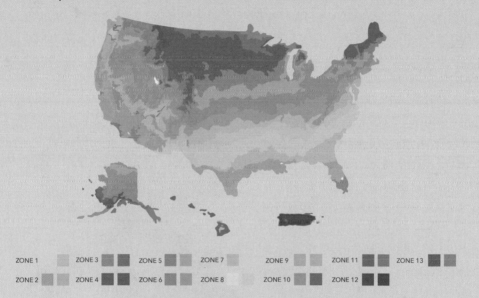

ZONE 1   ZONE 3   ZONE 5   ZONE 7   ZONE 9   ZONE 11   ZONE 13

ZONE 2   ZONE 4   ZONE 6   ZONE 8   ZONE 10   ZONE 12

For instance, a Meyer lemon tree is hardy in zones 9–11, whereas the honey crisp apple grows in zones 3–8. The adaptable (and native) choke cherry is hardy in zones 1–10.

Keep in mind that if a plant can be grown in a container, it can be moved inside for the winter and so grow in any zone. This is true of the Meyer lemon tree.

Note: The more common USDA map is the one used in this book. However, in Western states, some gardeners prefer the Sunset grow zone map, which accounts for additional factors, such as maximum average temperature, rainfall, humidity, and wind. If you live in the West, you can take advantage of the Sunset grow zone maps available online.

Besides your grow zone, it is important to know your region's first and last frost date. This is the average date—based on historical data—that the temperature dips to 32 degrees Fahrenheit (0 degrees Celsius) for the first or last time.

Because it is an average, the first and last frost may occur before or after the two dates in any given year. In fact, there is a 30 percent probability that the first frost will occur after your average first frost date, or that the last frost will occur before

your last frost date. For that reason, gardeners often plant frost-sensitive plants (like tomatoes) two weeks after the last frost date and fall crops (like fall and winter greens) two weeks before the first frost. (Fall plants can survive the frost, just not when they are first planted.) Spring plants that can withstand the occasional freeze of early spring can be planted well before the last frost date.

First and last frost dates also indicate the length of your growing season. The number of days between the two dates is the time available for growing annuals that cannot freeze. You can find the frost dates for your region by entering your city or town at the Old Farmers' Almanac website.

Mini Glossary

ANNUAL A plant that completes its life cycle in one year or less. Its seed is the only part of the plant that survives the growing season. Note that in much of America, some plants are grown as annuals but would live longer in a warmer climate. There are also some plants that "self-seed," meaning their seeds fall and then easily grow into new plants year after year.

Examples: peas, watermelons, zinnias

BIENNIAL A plant that completes its growing cycle in two years. Thereafter, the seed is the only part of the plant that survives. Some biennials are grown as annuals.

Examples: daisies, pansies, parsley

PERENNIAL A plant that lives more than two years. The term usually refers to nonwoody plants, as it is a given that trees and shrubs are perennials.

Examples: mint, blueberries, daylilies

For example, in Kansas City, Missouri, the last frost date is April 11, and the first frost date is October 28. The length of the growing season is, theoretically, 199 days. Remember, you'll want to plant two weeks after the last frost date, and then your plants may freeze two weeks before the first frost date. So your growing season may actually be 171 days. Still, that gives gardeners and farmers plenty of time to grow a wide variety of annuals.

Say, for instance, you're a gardener in Kansas City and you would like to grow Cherokee purple tomatoes. The harvest time is 85 days after planting. If you plant the seedlings (small plants grown from seeds) 14 days after the last frost date, you will still be left with 185 growing days, or 171 if the first frost comes early. After the harvest date, you have about 80–100 days of delicious tomatoes.

On the other hand, if you lived farther north in Duluth, Minnesota, your first frost date would be May 25, and the last frost date, September 22. Your grow season would be 119 days. Planting the Cherokee purple tomatoes 14 days after the last frost date, you'd be left with just 91–105 growing days and 6–20 days of tomatoes. For short grow seasons, you'd want to plant Early Girl tomatoes, which are ready to be harvested in 50 days, leaving 41–55 days of tomatoes.

Vegetable Planting Calendar

| JAN | FEB | MARCH | APRIL | MAY | JUNE | JULY | AUG | SEPT | OCT | NOV | DEC |

Room to Grow

Plants need room to grow. Their branches and leaves must be able to spread out into the sunlight, and their roots need space to soak up nutrients and water from the soil undeterred by rocks, hardscape (bricks, asphalt, concrete, etc.), or other plants. If forced to waste energy jockeying for space, plants won't have energy left to produce flowers and fruit. Plants also need space for the air to circulate around them so that they can dry out after a rainfall, avoiding fungal growth. Finally, it's important that plants not touch each other, lest flightless pests easily hop from one to the other.

The room needed by each plant varies widely. While radishes need just two or three inches per plant, a tomato needs three feet, and a sweet cherry tree requires twenty-five feet!

2-3"   3-4'   25'

There are ways to conserve space while giving plants ample room. First, trees and large plants can often tolerate smaller plants growing between them—strawberries between cherry trees or radishes between tomato plants, for instance. Second, dwarf varieties that require less space are available for many plants and trees, and they naturally grow smaller in containers. Container plants have an added advantage. In a pot, they don't require as much soil square footage as they would in the ground because the roots are not competing for water and nutrients. However, their roots need enough room inside the container so that they don't spill out (and dry up in the air), and the plants must be spaced so that their branches don't touch.

Row by Row or Block by Block

Plants can be grown in rows—straight lines with more space in between the rows than the plants in the line, or in blocks—squares in which each plant is spaced equally. Oftentimes, rows are used for larger spaces. They are convenient in that you can walk between rows, add mulch, and weed with a hoe. For smaller spaces, block planting is more efficient. Keep in mind that you'll need to get to every plant. Small squares surrounded by pathways make this possible.

Water

All plants need water, though the amount varies. Some like to be watered daily, and others rarely. There are also plants that need to be watered heavily but then dry out before the next watering. If your region is extremely wet or dry, you'll want to select plants that can withstand that extreme. Native plants are a sure bet, as they are uniquely adapted to your climate, do not require a great deal of care, and provide food and shelter to the native animals that evolved alongside them.

On the other hand, water can be adjusted to some extent. You can't stop the rain, of course, and in rain forest regions, you'll need to select plants adapted to being nearly constantly wet. But if a plant needs more water than your regional rainfall provides, that is easily done. First, be aware of any watering restrictions (common in drought-prone regions) that may limit your ability to water a garden. Also, to conserve water, consider using a rain barrel to catch rainfall

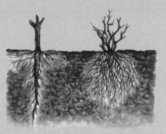

for later watering. Finally, make sure your plants get the most out of the water you provide.

A plant absorbs water from the soil through its roots. The longer the soil can hold water, the more the plant can absorb. Plan to water your garden in the cool of the morning, when less water will evaporate because of heat. Second, plant water-loving varieties in plastic containers, which retain moisture better than pottery. For in-ground gardens, consider your native soil. Sandy soil drains quickly and will need to be adapted for water-loving plants. For more information, see chapter 3.

When to Water

Plants' water needs vary. In this book, they are labeled as needing moderate water, heavy water, or light water. These labels are often given in lieu of stating how frequently the plant should be watered, because that varies according to the temperature and whether the plant is in the ground or a container. Whereas watering once a week may be fine for gardeners with mild summers, it's not nearly enough if you have hot summers. During a heat wave, you may even need

to water every day. Also, plants in containers require more water because A) their roots can't reach deep into the soil to find moisture reserves, and B) they get hotter because they are not cooled by the ground below. Moreover, terra-cotta and stone containers require at least twice as frequent watering as plastic containers.

Here's what the labels mean:

MODERATE WATER ▸ Most plants require moderate water. Think about your own feelings about water—you probably like going for a swim, but not walking around in wet shoes. Likewise, these plants like to be watered when their roots are dry, but they don't like their roots sitting in water. For plants requiring a moderate amount of water, a good rule of thumb is to water whenever the soil is dry an inch deep. If the plant's leaves start to shrivel, that is a telltale sign that it needs to be watered—and watered more often moving forward. So about how often will this be? It depends on your weather. If your summers are mild (with highs around 70–80°F), once a week is probably fine for in-ground plants, twice a week for plastic-container plants, and every other day for earthenware-container plants. If your summers are hot (with highs around 90), you'll need to water every few days for in-ground plants and every day for plants in containers. If your highs are hotter than that, your plants will require daily or even twice daily water, and some afternoon shade. When you do water, water deeply—the equivalent of an inch of rain. That's about one gallon per square foot. (To test how long you should water your garden with a hose, time how long it takes to fill an empty gallon container with water from the hose. Multiply the time by the number of square feet in your garden. Now you can water your garden for that amount of time, moving the hose around so that it is watered evenly.) Keep in mind that plants may require more water when producing fruit. Watch for shriveled leaves, and up your watering frequency if needed.

HEAVY WATER While these plants can also be damaged by too much water, they don't like drying out in between watering. They should be watered whenever the top of the soil feels dry. In hot climates, they'll also benefit from afternoon shade—even if they require full sun. In regions with mild summers, these plants will need to be watered every few days. During hot summers, they need to be watered every day. They are not well suited for extreme heat or dry climates. In containers, they should be watered once or twice a day.

LIGHT WATER Plants requiring light water need only be watered during droughts outside or every one to four weeks inside. Exception: If you live in a desert climate, you'll need to water at least once a week—whether the plant is inside or outside.

Nutrients

Plants need nutrients to live. The nutrients are dissolved in the water the plants absorb. Nutrients start out in the soil and originate from once-living things, also called organic matter. These nutrients are recycled from living thing to living thing. First, plants absorb and store the nutrients. Animals, in turn, eat the plants and absorb the nutrients. Animals excrete some of the nutrients and store others. When the plants or animals die and decompose, the nutrients go back into the soil. The soil in your yard has some nutrients in it. This would be enough for native plants, which have adapted to this soil, and weeds, which grow easily in a variety of soils (that's why they are weeds!). However, your garden plants may need extra nutrients.

To increase the nutrients in soil, you must add organic matter or synthetic fertilizer. Both contain three chemicals important to plant growth and health: nitrogen, phosphate, and potassium. In synthetic fertilizer, the chemicals have been formulated by scientists. Organic matter contains the chemicals naturally. Examples include manure (animal poop), compost (decayed plant matter), bonemeal (from ground bones), fish emulsion (from fish parts), and liquid seaweed. The manure, bonemeal, and fish emulsion contain nutrients from the plants eaten by the animals, and the compost and seaweed contain nutrients from the plants themselves. Besides fertilizing the plants, organic matter also feeds helpful bacteria in the soil. Organic matter can be purchased at a garden store or made at home by composting your kitchen scraps. (Learn how on page 36.)

Bunny Poop

Rabbit droppings are said to be the best all-round fertilizer. Dry and odorless, they are easy to store and can be added to the garden at any time. You may be able to find a neighbor with a pet rabbit whose pellets you could collect each week. One rabbit pal will be plenty. A single rabbit produces roughly enough poop for a 500-square-foot (46.5-square-meter) garden.

CHAPTER 2

Garden Plants and Supplies

Now that you know what a plant needs, it's time to think about what you need for your garden. That includes making a budget and deciding which supplies and plants to buy.

Budget

Apart from the needs of the plant, your own budget should be considered. Garden costs include seeds or seedlings (young plants), potting soil or garden soil, mulch, fertilizer, containers, tools, and garden structures such as trellises.

PUMPKIN SEEDS

Some plants can be grown as seeds sown directly into the soil, whereas others should be grown from a seedling or other small plant. Seedlings are more expensive than seeds. You can grow your own seedlings inside and then transplant them, but that is considered a more advanced gardening skill.

TOMATO PLANT SEEDLING

Seeds, Seedlings, and More

All plants can be grown from a seed. However, not all plants should be grown from a seed in the garden. For one thing, the grow season may be too short to allow for a seed to grow into a mature plant. Or maybe those seeds make a tasty meal for a rodent and are likely to get dug up immediately. In these cases (and more), you may want to purchase seedlings—young plants grown from seeds.

In some cases, there is an easier way to propagate a plant than a seed. If you can grow your plant from a cutting (the branch)—such as mint, a sprout (sometimes called a slip or eye, as in sweet potatoes and potatoes), or an offset (a plant that is reproduced by a parent plant and grows beside it—often in bulb form) such as a tulip, then you are further along in the growth process than starting with a seed.

MINT CUTTING

TULIP OFFSET

Finally, some plants grown from seed do not turn out like their parents. For instance, apple trees grown from apple seeds do not bear the same kind of apples as their parent tree, so they are grown from cuttings grafted onto a hardy rootstock (a system of roots that can survive disease and pests).

SWEET POTATO
SPROUT/SLIP/EYE

Sow Many Seeds

If you do grow a plant from seeds, you'll want to sow more seeds than the number of plants you want to end up with—typically a few seeds every few inches. As they grow, you will "thin" the plants, removing the smaller seedlings so that the others have more room. Use scissors to snip them at their base so that you do not disturb the soil. See plant descriptions for the space ultimately needed between plants.

Second, you'll need potting mix for containers or garden soil for raised beds, and nutrients in the form of organic matter or other fertilizer. For an in-ground garden, the soil is already there, but you'll likely need to add organic matter. For a raised bed, container garden, or plants that need support, you'll need containers and garden structures. They can be expensive but don't have to be. You can reduce costs by shopping garage sales, using lower-cost supplies (buckets instead of planters, for instance), or upcycling household items.

One flip side to the cost of gardening: If you grow food, you may see your family grocery bill drop!

Plant Classification

All plants belong to the plant kingdom. Within that kingdom, each plant belongs to a phylum, class, order, family, genus, and species, with each category becoming narrower. Within a species there are varieties, or cultivars, with different traits, such as size, color, and flavor. For instance, tomato is a species, but within the species there are several varieties/cultivars, ranging from cherry tomatoes to large beefsteak tomatoes. Sometimes, the term cultivar is used to differentiate cultivated varieties from varieties found in the wild.

In the garden, less attention is paid to how plants are classified than how plants are known. Some plants are thought of as a genus (lilies), others as a species (tomatoes), and still others as a variety (cabbage). In this book plant descriptions are given based on how that plant is best known. Suggested varieties/cultivars are given in most cases, or else similar species.

Broader grouping	**Kingdom** ±280,000 species	**Plantae** (plants)
	Phylum ±250,000 species	**Angiospermae** (flowering plants)
	Class ±235,000 species	**Dicotyledonae** (dicots)
	Order ±18,000 species	**Rosales** (rosses and other allies)
Narrower grouping	**Family** ±3,500 species	**Rosaceae** (rose family)
	Genus ±500 species	**Rosa**
	Species Beach rose	**Rosa rugosa**

Tools

Tools make gardening more convenient. But don't worry if you don't have all the tools on this list! You can make do with what you have. A spoon can replace the trowel, buckets can replace a wheelbarrow, and a shovel can be used to till, dig, and mulch.

- **WHEELBARROW** to move soil and mulch
- **TILLER/CULTIVATOR** to prepare the soil for an in-ground garden
- **TROWEL** to plant seeds and seedlings
- **BUCKET** to move materials
- **HOE** to weed between rows
- **SPADE/SHOVEL** to move soil, compost, and fertilizer; work soil; and plant seedlings and larger plants
- **FORK** to move mulch and compost
- **SAW** to prune bushes and trees
- **SNIPS** to prune small branches and small plants
- **SOD CUTTER** to cut and remove sod
- **FLOWER RAKE** to harvest flowers from herbs
- **GARDENING GLOVES** to protect your hands from small scrapes and sticky plant oils. (For extra prickly plants, try cut-resistant gloves.)

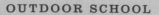

CHAPTER 3

Container Gardens

A garden doesn't have to be a plot of land. It can be a collection of pots—or any other type of container. There are several reasons to have a container garden. First, your outdoor space (and sun) may be limited to hard surfaces such as a balcony, deck, or rooftop. Second, if you do have a yard, the soil may be poor. You can fix the soil by adding organic material and other materials, but a container garden is less time-consuming for beginners. Third, you may want to move perennials or small trees indoors for the winter, and that's possible if they are grown in pots. Finally, some plants are best suited for pots. For instance, mint will take over a garden if planted in the ground, so it is best contained.

For a container garden, there are four factors to consider: what to plant, what kind of containers to use, what kind of potting mix to use, and finally, where to put the containers.

What to Plant

Think your dream garden is too big for pots? Are you envisioning an apple orchard? Lemon grove? Pumpkin patch? Believe it or not, all those plants can be grown in containers. In fact, nearly any plant that can grow in the ground can also grow in a container. Just be sure to choose dwarf or patio varieties for large plants or trees.

When choosing plants, think about whether you can meet their basic needs. With container gardens, you are better able to control the environment than you can with in-ground gardens. You can select a larger container for a plant that needs more room to grow, move the plant inside during cold or hot weather, water the plant appropriately, provide nutrients in the potting mix, and even move the pot throughout the day for optimum sunlight (though you may not want this daily chore). It may seem like the sky is the limit for container gardens, but you are still limited by your budget and the amount of space you have for containers.

Patio or dwarf varieties of large plants will naturally grow to the size supported by their smaller root systems. For trees, the canopy (the system of leaves and branches) will be much larger than the root system. A dwarf tree's canopy may span 12 feet (3.5 meters) at its widest. If your outdoor space is not that big, or you don't want that much shade for your other plants, a tree is not a good fit. Interestingly, some fruit trees have columnar varieties that grow up in a straight line, so that the canopy spans just 2 feet (61 cm)!

For your budget, the cost of the garden will increase with every container. Even if you find a free container to repurpose, you'll still need to purchase or make potting mix and then purchase the plants themselves. In general, trees and perennials cost more than other plants but save money in the long run since they return year after year. Seedlings cost more than seeds, so any plant you can grow from seed will cost less. Finally, smaller plants tend to cost less than larger plants, and the same is true of small containers. In short, the smaller your garden and plants, the less it will cost to get started.

Container Garden Ideas

FOUR CORNERS ORCHARD
Grow a container fruit tree in each corner of your outdoor space.

BERRY PATCH Grow berry bushes in a row.

BLUEBERRY RASPBERRY BLACKBERRY

RATATOU-YAY Grow vegetables in different size pots.

FLORIBUNDA Grow perennial flowers in an oversize flower box.

SUCCULENT Grow a succulent centerpiece.

TRY IT →

Grow Green Onions from Kitchen Scraps

Green onions add crunch and flavor to any savory dish. Why not grow your own from scraps?

WHAT YOU'LL NEED

➢ scissors or knife, 1-pint (0.5-L) jar or cup, water, and 1–12 green onions

STEP 1 Fill the jar with 2 inches (5 cm) of water.

STEP 2 Cut the green onions where the green begins.

STEP 3 Place the white part of the green onions' root side down in the water. Place the jar in a sunny window.

STEP 4 Change the water every day.

STEP 5 The green onions will show growth after just one day. When the green part is 6 inches (15 cm) long, you can harvest the green part and use it. It will grow again!

I DID IT! DATE:

WHAT YOU'LL NEED

➢ 2 inches of garden space per green onion, 1 or more green onions, and scissors or knife

STEP 1 Cut the green onions where the green begins.

STEP 2 Dig 1-inch (2.5-cm) holes, 2 inches (5 cm) apart.

STEP 3 Plant the green onions, root down, in the holes, making sure the roots are covered. Plant 2 inches (5 cm) apart. Water every day.

STEP 4 The green onions will show growth after just one day. When the green part is 6 inches (15 cm) long, you can harvest the green part and use it. It will grow again! Green onions are perennials. As long as you leave the root in the ground, they will grow back each spring!

I DID IT! DATE:

What Kind of Containers?

When choosing a container, first consider the size. Containers are measured by the volume they hold or the diameter across the top of the pot. Volume is more precise, as diameter is just one dimension of a container. Most plants need containers between 1 and 15 gallons (4–57 liters) in volume. Small vegetables and herbs are fine in a 1-gallon (4-L) container—or even smaller in some cases. For perennials, bushes, and trees, start with small containers and "pot up"—transplant it to a larger pot—every year or two. You want to avoid having the plant become root bound—with roots growing around the inner edge or out the bottom of the pot. So if you can see its roots through the opening at the bottom of the pot, it is time to pot up.

Why not just start with a large pot in the first place? Large pots retain more water. A young plant doesn't absorb that much water, and its roots may become soggy and rotten. Also, plants like to be snuggled in, to some extent. Think of them in the wild, growing in between rocks and roots, as opposed to all alone in a large expanse of soil.

In the end, a 15-gallon (56.5 liter) container will be big enough for the largest plant or full-grown dwarf tree. Of course, there are many sizes in between. The ideal container size can be determined by the plant's space requirement, as shown below. Keep in mind that small plants can share a large container. In that case, the depth of a large container is not needed. To conserve potting mix, you can fill the bottom of the pot with plastic bottles or repurposed Styrofoam.

How Big Should the Container Be?

SPACE REQUIRED	CONTAINER SIZE	SAMPLE PLANTS
6 inches or less (15 cm)	1 gallon (4 L)	lettuce, small herbs, radish, strawberry
12–18 inches (30.5–45.5 cm)	7 gallon (26.5 L)	collard greens, cabbages, large herbs
24 inches or more (61 cm)	15 gallon (56.5 L)	eggplant, tomatoes, pumpkins, trees

Climbing Plants in Pots

Climbing plants need a structure on which to grow beyond the container. The structure can be set in the container, beside it, or between two containers. You can also use structures that already exist in your outdoor space. For instance, you can grow a plant up a fence or over a wall.

Tomato with cage inside the pot.

A bean plant in a pot with a trellis.

Two vining squash plants in large containers with an archway in between.

Next consider the material of the containers. In garden shops, common materials for planters are concrete, earthenware, wood, plastic, weatherproof metal, and fabric. Concrete is durable but very heavy. It's not a good fit for a plant that needs to be moved or rests on any structure other than a ground-level patio. Earthenware is made of natural material, such as clay, and then fired. It has a beautiful natural look, and plants like it because it dries out faster, preventing their roots from getting waterlogged. However, it is fairly heavy—and breakable. Weatherproof metal, wood, and plastic are all lighter weight. If you use plastic garden materials, look for ways to recycle them to keep them out of the plastic waste stream. Many garden centers and organizations collect plastic to be reused. Fabric grow bags are another option. They are made of biodegradable fabric, which is lightweight and porous so that the plants don't get waterlogged.

	CONCRETE	EARTHENWARE	WOOD	PLASTIC	METAL	FABRIC
PRO	durable	natural material/look breathable	lightweight	lightweight	weather proof, lightweight	lightweight, porous, and bio-degradable
CON	heavy	heavy and breakable	shorter lifespan, can rot	create plastic waste	can overheat in sun	

ECO-FRIENDLY

As a home design item, garden pots can be expensive. To save money, use containers known more for their function than beauty: buckets, troughs, or barrels. Better yet, search your house, thrift stores, and garage sales, not only for traditional garden containers but also for anything big and sturdy enough for a plant.

You can even use the potting mix bag itself! Make holes in the bottom for water drainage. Then lay the bag on its side. Cut four equal size squares. Plant strawberries, lettuce, or small herbs in each square.

Upcycled Garden Containers

hollow tree stump

baby pool

wooden drawer

wheelbarrow

sink

colander

tire

rubber rain boots

fabric shoe holder

reusable grocery bag

large ice cream tub

storage container

PRO TIPS

➣ Use outdoor paint to add color or uniformity. Painting all containers white creates both a clean look and keeps plants cooler in hot climates.

➣ If the container is solid, drill holes at the bottom so that excess water can spill out.

What Potting Mix to Use

Plants grown in the ground benefit from the natural water cycle. Rainwater dampens the soil and then excess water drains down into the water table below. As long as the soil has adequate drainage, plant roots do not become waterlogged. On the other hand, containers, despite their drainage holes, trap water, posing the danger of too-wet roots. That can cause disease. In addition, soil can become compacted in a container, squashing roots so that they can no longer take up water or nutrients. For these reasons, container plants require a different growing medium than in-ground plants. Potting mix is the best option. It dries out faster than garden soil so that plants don't get too much water. Because of this, container plants need to be watered more often than in-ground plants. The idea is to provide plants with regular water—but not too much all at once. Potting mix is also less dense than garden soil, so it doesn't compact in the close quarters of a container and crush plant roots.

COARSE SAND (BUILDER'S SAND)

PEAT MOSS

COCO FIBER

ECO-FRIENDLY

What exactly is potting mix? It's a lightweight mixture of various ingredients. Together, the ingredients should provide the plant with structural stability, room for the roots to grow, adequate drainage, and good nutrition (though that can be added separately). A typical mix would include peat moss or coco fiber; perlite, vermiculite, or sand; and nutrients in the form of organic matter or fertilizer. It may also include some garden soil. Peat moss is moss that has been decomposing in airless bogs for thousands of years. It is lightweight but still able to retain water and nutrients and release them slowly. The mining of peat moss releases carbon into the environment, so some people prefer coco fiber, a by-product of coconuts that has qualities like peat moss. It is more eco-friendly but also more expensive. Perlite is superheated volcanic rock. Vermiculite is a mineral. Sand is a collection of rock fragments. All three help with airflow and drainage and provide weight to the mix while still allowing drainage and preventing compaction.

COARSE SAND

PEATMOSS

COCO FIBER

COMPOST

TRY IT →

Make Your Own Potting Soil

WHAT YOU'LL NEED

➤ coarse sand, peat moss or coco fiber, compost, a large container for mixing, a trowel (optional), and pot or pots for the finished potting soil

STEP 1 Add one part coarse sand (builder's sand), one part peat moss or coco fiber, and one part compost to the container.

STEP 2 Stir with the trowel or your hands.

STEP 3 Place the mixture in the pot or pots, leaving 2 inches (5 cm) at the top.

STEP 4 Add water to dampen before adding plants.

I DID IT! DATE:

Make Your Own Compost

You can make your own compost. The compost heap can be as simple as a pile of kitchen and yard waste that you mix with a shovel or as high tech as a barrel with a crank to turn it.

> **WHAT YOU'LL NEED**
>
> ➤ yard or kitchen waste; a 1-gallon container, lidded or sealable (such as a crock, Tupperware, or ziplock bag); dry items: dead leaves, newspaper, or sawdust; an out-of-the-way spot in the yard

STEP 1 Dump yard waste such as leaves and grass (but not weeds with seeds) into the compost heap.

STEP 2 Collect fruit and vegetable scraps in the container.

STEP 3 When the container is full, add it to the compost heap.

STEP 4 Once you have a full layer of kitchen scraps evenly spread over the compost heap, add a dry layer, such as dead leaves, newspaper, or sawdust. You can dampen it with hose water so that it doesn't blow away. Then begin the process of adding kitchen scraps again.

STEP 5 To speed the compost process, water the heap and turn it with a shovel once a week.

STEP 6 When it's ready, the compost will look like thick, dark soil.

I DID IT! DATE:

How to Arrange the Containers

When your containers are ready, arrange them in a way that is practical and appealing. Often, containers are placed around the perimeter of a patio, porch, or deck. Note that for balconies and rooftops, the edge is most structurally strong, so this is the best place for containers. If you only have a few pots, you may want to place them in the corners, or next to each seating spot. Sunny spots will also dictate where to put the containers (see the "Sunlight" section in chapter 1). Unless you plan to play musical chairs with your pots, choose a spot that is consistently sunny and make sure large plants don't shade the smaller ones.

CHAPTER 4

A Small-Plot Garden

A small-plot garden grows in the ground or in a raised bed. In chapters 1 and 2, you learned what a plant needs and gathered your supplies, and in chapter 3 you grew some plants in containers. Now it's time to make some final decisions, prepare the space, and put those new gardening skills to use.

The Shape of Things

First, decide the shape, location, and size of your garden. Your garden can be any shape, but rectangle, square, circle, or part of a circle are most common. A rectangle is often chosen because it can run along the fence line, patio, or house without cutting too far into the rest of your yard. The fence or wall can then provide scaffolding for large or climbing plants. Finally, a rectangle provides easy access to all plants for weeding and watering.

A corner, a square, or a quarter circle is just as practical if you simply leave a pathway to access the corner-most plants.

If space is not an issue, a full circle or square allows you to plan your garden around a pretty focal point.

The size of your garden depends on how much space is available, how many plants you want to grow, how much time you are willing to spend, and your budget for purchasing plants and other supplies. It's a good idea to start small, but in a location with adjacent space available for expansion.

TRACK IT ↘

What Is Your Garden Vision?

In Parts II–VI of this book, you will find descriptions like the sample below of plants in the herb and spice, vegetable, fruit, flower, and "other" categories. They will include growing instructions. Browse the plants described in this book. Make a list of 10 plants you'd like to grow and can grow, based on the plant's needs.

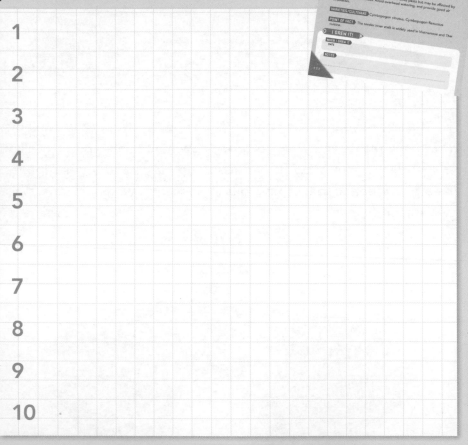

1

2

3

4

5

6

7

8

9

10

I DID IT!   DATE:

Now create a map of your garden. This will help you determine how many plants to purchase and where to plant them for optimum growth.

STEP 1 Narrow your list of 10 plants down to 2–5. This is plenty for a beginner garden. You can add more later.

STEP 2 Use the rectangle provided or draw the shape that you intend for your garden. Each square equals one square foot.

STEP 3 Draw the plant or plants that you plan to grow there.

I DID IT! DATE:

Prepare the Soil (or Don't)

The final decision is whether to dig an in-ground garden or build a raised-bed garden. First, consider the type and quality of your soil. Soil is the top layer of Earth's crust. It is a combination of decayed things that used to be alive, rock particles, and still living things. Soil differs greatly from place to place. The three main types of soil you'll find in a garden are clay, silt, and sand. There is also peat, but you're unlikely to come across it. (In the peat fields where it's found, it's mined for the peat moss used in potting mix.) Most soil is a mixture of clay, silt, and sand, with one being predominant. Loam refers to an ideal soil mixture for growing plants. If you have loamy soil, you are in luck! You only need to add nutrients to make your plants happy.

State of the Soil

Soil Composition: Sand (%)

0   20   40   60   80   100

Soil Composition: Silt (%)

0   10 20 30 40 50 60 70

Soil Composition: Clay (%)

0   10 20 30 40 50 60

Look at the maps. If your region on the sand map is dark brown, the soil tends to be sandy. If the region on the silt map is dark pink, it is silty. If there's a dark blue region on the clay map, it is clay. As you can see, soil type varies by region. The East Coast tends toward sandy soil, which is understandable given its location by the ocean. The sandy region in the middle of the country is the Nebraska sandhills, 19,300 square miles (49,987 square km) of dunes covered by vegetation. The Mississippi River Valley and much of the upper Midwest tend toward silty soil because of deposits from glacial melt at the end of the ice age, and more recently, deposits from the river. Clay is especially common in Texas but can be found throughout the country. These are generalizations, and soil varies quite a bit from place to place. Your local garden organizations or university extension will have insight into the soil in your area.

Over thousands of years, native plants have adapted to the soil in their region. With enough rain, sun, and room to grow, they thrive in that soil. However, for nonnative plants, you usually need to change the soil to fit their needs. To do that, you must know your soil type, its pluses and minuses, how to adapt it to suit the needs of your plants, and when to forget about your native soil and build a raised bed.

Clay

How to tell if you have clay soil: If your soil becomes rock hard, and even cracked, when dry, and very heavy when wet, you likely have clay soil.

The good: Clay soil retains water well, and with it, nutrients.

The bad: Clay soil is easily compacted, making it hard for roots to grow. Breaking up clay so that it has better aeration is backbreaking labor.

What to do: The easiest way to deal with clay soil . . . is not to. Raised beds are best if you have this soil type. If you really want to have an in-ground garden, rent or borrow a motorized tiller. While you till the soil, mix in compost to aerate (add air to) the soil and add nutrients. Do not add sand, because this can cause clay soil to turn into concrete.

Silt

How to tell if you have silty soil: If your soil feels soft and almost floury when dry, and smooth and silky when wet, and if it can be made into a ball when damp, then you have silty soil.

The good: Silty soil is very fertile. It retains water and nutrients well.

The bad: Silty soil can easily be compacted, damaging roots. It can also become waterlogged.

What to do: Till the soil with a motorized tiller, or when it is dry, with a pitchfork. Add organic matter to aerate the soil and add nutrients. Then avoid walking on your garden beds. Form paths in your garden from which you can reach your plants.

Sand

How to tell if you have sandy soil: This is the easiest soil to recognize. It looks and feels like the sand on a beach!

The good: Sandy soil is lightweight and easy to work with. That means it's easy to mix materials into the soil to improve it.

The bad: Sandy soil drains easily, meaning plants can dry out. With the water, the plants also lose their nutrients.

What to do: Till the soil with a pitchfork or motorized tiller. Add lots of compost to add nutrients and help with water retention. Around large plants or trees also add mulch, which will retain water and add further nutrients to the soil.

Acidic or Basic Soil

Whatever the type, soil also has a pH level. The pH scale ranges from 0 to 14 and describes how substances react when they are dissolved in water. Distilled water has a pH of 7. A substance with a pH higher than 7 is a base, and a pH lower than 7, an acid. Many of the foods we eat are weak acids or bases. For instance, lemon juice is an acid, and eggs are a base. Stronger acids and bases cannot be consumed. They include battery acid (an acid) and bleach (a base).

Soil can be neutral, acidic, or basic. Most garden plants prefer neutral soil, but it doesn't have to be exactly neutral. They will thrive in soils with pH of 5.5–7.5. If the pH level is higher or lower than that, many plants have trouble absorbing nutrients. If you use potting mix or garden soil, it will fall well within the near-neutral range. For in-ground soil, check with your local garden organization, garden store, or university extension to see if your region is known to have acidic or basic soil. If there is cause for concern, use a pH soil tester to find out.

Soil may become acidic because of organic matter breaking down and reacting to water in the soil. It can become basic because of chalk and lime—soft rocks in the soil that are bases and easily erode. If your soil test shows that the soil is too acidic, you can add lime. If your soil test shows that the soil is too basic, you can add organic matter. If your soil is too acidic or basic, you may also choose to build a raised-bed garden.

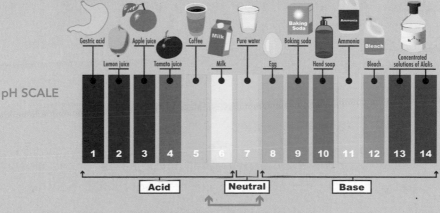

Test Your Soil

Acids such as vinegar and bases such as baking soda react with each other, releasing gas (bubbles) as they do. You'll use both to test your soil. This test shows whether your soil is basic or acidic, but not how basic or acidic. Plants can grow in slightly basic and acidic soils. If you are concerned that your soil is too extreme either way, purchase a more precise testing kit.

> **WHAT YOU'LL NEED**
>
> ➢ 0.5-cup measuring cup, 1-cup measuring cup, two small bowls, 0.5 cup of vinegar, and 0.5 cup of baking soda

STEP 1 Scoop 1 cup of soil from your garden. For the most accurate results, take the soil from a few places in the garden.

STEP 2 Mix the soil and then divide it between the two bowls.

STEP 3 Add 0.5 cup of water to each bowl.

STEP 4 Add 0.5 cup of vinegar to one of the bowls. If the vinegar bubbles, you have basic soil.

STEP 5 Add 0.5 cup of baking soda to the other bowl. If it bubbles, your soil is acidic.

The weaker the bubbles, whether acidic or basic, the closer to neutral your soil is. If there are no bubbles, your soil is neutral.

I DID IT!   DATE:

Reasons to Make a Raised-Bed Garden

Your soil is clay.

Your soil shows signs of being poor quality: No vegetation grows there. For instance, it is too basic or acidic, or it is nutrient poor.

You don't have access to a motorized tiller. (In sandy soil, you probably don't need one.)

You like the look of a raised-bed garden.

Garden Soil

Garden soil (sometimes called topsoil) is soil that you purchase. The quality of soil available for sale varies widely depending on its past use. Topsoil left over from a construction project, for instance, may not have the nutrients and qualities your plants need. Garden soil has been mixed to create an ideal environment for plants. It will include organic matter found naturally in healthy soil, but probably not enough for your garden plants. For more complete nutrients, add compost to the garden soil. Compost can be made at home (see chapter 2) or purchased from garden suppliers. You can likely buy it from your soil company or even have it mixed into your soil. You can add additional fertilizer (see chapter 1) before planting.

Why Not Use Potting Mix in a Raised Bed?

Potting mix is used instead of soil in containers so that they do not become waterlogged. Raised beds, on the other hand, drain down into the soil, so overwatering is not as much of a problem. They also tend to be larger and have a larger surface area than most containers, so constantly keeping the potting mix damp would be nearly impossible.

Soil Safari

You know that soil contains earthworms, millipedes, and ants, but on a microscopic level, it has so much more. A teaspoon (one gram) of soil can have one billion bacteria. Other small life forms include fungus, protozoa, and roundworms. They break down nutrients, enabling plants to absorb them, make the soil better able to hold water, and even produce antibiotics, helping plants to stay healthy. Adding organic matter to soil feeds not only the plants directly but also the tiny living things in the soil so that they can better support your plants over time.

Planting Your Garden

When you've chosen the location, shape, and size of your garden, it's time to prepare and plant it. You can either till the soil and plant an in-ground garden or add garden soil for a raised garden. If your soil is workable, an in-ground garden is fine. Just add nutrients such as manure as you till it with a motorized tiller or pitchfork. If your soil is poor or difficult to work, then a raised garden is better. Create a perimeter with stones or bricks and add garden soil in the middle.

Once the soil is ready, you can plant your garden. For seeds, you will plant more than the amount that will actually mature. There is a saying: "One for the mouse, one for the crow, one to rot, one to grow." It means that not all seeds survive, and that is why you plant extra. Some seeds do best with broadcast sowing, meaning you spread the seeds consistently along the row. For others, you will plant a few seeds every few inches. Both methods ensure that even if some seeds never sprout, others will still grow. Either way, you will want to draw a line with your finger, sprinkle on the seeds, and then cover the seeds with a little soil. When the seeds sprout, let them grow two leaves. Then you can thin them according to the directions so that they have the space they truly need. The best way to do this is to snip the unwanted plants close to their base. That way, you do not disturb the soil.

For seedlings, the assumption is that all will survive, so space them according to how much room they need to grow throughout their lifetimes. You can follow the directions provided by the seller or the ones found in this book. Draw row lines in the soil with your garden tool and dig small holes so that the seedlings' roots will be underground, but the stems and leaves above ground.

After planting everything, water the garden. This holds the seeds and seedlings in place and gives the garden a good start. Continue to water (following the instructions in the book for heavy, moderate, or light water). Also weed your garden so that your plants are not competing for space, sunlight, and nutrients.

A SMALL-PLOT GARDEN

For an in-ground garden:

WHAT YOU'LL NEED

➤ tape measure, seeds and seedlings, spoon or spade, compost, water, twine, tarp or trash bag; 4 bricks or stones; shovel; sod cutter; motorized tiller or pitchfork; hoe or rake

STEP 1 Measure the space with a tape measure and mark the edges with twine.

STEP 2 Pull up any weeds by their roots.

STEP 3 Remove or kill other vegetation. To kill the current vegetation, lay a tarp or trash bag over the area and weigh it down in each corner with bricks or stones. Leave it there for a month. Then the dead plants can be tilled into the soil as organic matter. Otherwise, remove plants with a shovel and thick grass with a sod cutter.

STEP 4 Till the soil a foot (30.5 cm) deep using a motorized tiller or pitchfork.

STEP 5 Add 4 inches (10 cm) of compost or other organic matter. Till this into the soil.

STEP 6 Use a hoe or rake to level the soil.

STEP 7 Bring your seeds and seedlings outside.

STEP 8 Check your map to see where each plant will go.

STEP 9 For the first plant, review the planting instructions.

STEP 10 Draw a line with your finger or garden tool where you will plant the seeds or seedlings. For seeds, follow the directions on the seed packet or in this book. Cover the seeds with a little soil and then move on to the next planting.

STEP 11 For seedlings, follow the spacing recommended on the plant tag or in this book. Dig a small hole—just slightly larger than the root ball. Plant the seedling. Fill the gaps in the hole with soil and cover the root ball with a small amount of soil.

STEP 12 Water right away, and then according to directions.

For a raised-bed garden:

WHAT YOU'LL NEED

➢ tape measure, seeds and seedlings, spoon or spade, compost, water, blocks, railroad ties or other perimeters; wheelbarrow; garden soil; shovel or garden fork

STEP 1 Measure the space with a tape measure and mark the edges.

STEP 2 Place blocks, railroad ties, or another perimeter around the space. Using a wheelbarrow and shovel, dump garden soil and compost to fill the space. Mix it with a shovel or garden fork. (Note: Garden soil and compost are sold in cubic feet or yards. To figure out how much you need (total), multiply the length, width, and depth of the space. Say your garden is 4 feet long, 2 feet wide, and 8 inches deep. You will need 5.3 cubic feet of garden soil + compost, or 2.15 cubic feet each.)

STEP 3 Bring your seeds and seedlings outside.

STEP 4 Check your map to see where each plant will go.

STEP 5 For the first plant, review the planting instructions.

STEP 6 Draw a line with your finger or garden tool where you will plant the seeds or seedlings. For seeds, follow the directions on the seed packet or in this book. Cover the seeds with a little soil and then move on to the next planting.

STEP 7 For seedlings, follow the spacing recommended on the plant tag or in this book. Dig a small hole—just slightly larger than the root ball. Plant the seedling. Fill the gaps in the hole with soil and cover the root ball with a small amount of soil.

STEP 8 Water right away, and then according to directions.

I DID IT! DATE:

Measuring

When it comes to planting, you can estimate by using two fingers for an inch (2.5 cm), or the length of your palm for 6 inches (15 cm).

Sample Small-Plot Gardens

VEGETABLE GARDEN tomatoes, lettuce, zucchini on a vine, carrots

FRUIT GARDEN apple tree with strawberries growing underneath, a berry bush

HERB GARDEN parsley, sage, rosemary, thyme

FLOWER GARDEN rose bush, daisies, chrysanthemums

CACTUS GARDEN aloe, prickly pear, cereus, ferocactus

LITTLE OF EVERYTHING GARDEN apple tree with tulips growing underneath; small herbs in a row, tomatoes and zucchini

CHAPTER 5

Troubleshooting

Gardening is not without its challenges. Pests and disease can kill the plants you worked hard to grow. The best way to deal with trouble is to avoid it. By providing appropriate sunlight, temperature, space, water, and nutrients, you will go a long way in preventing pests and disease. That's because healthy plants can defend themselves to some extent.

Healthy roots, stems, and leaves make it difficult for insects and germs (microscopic organisms that cause disease) to make their way inside the plant. If they do get in, plants can release toxic chemicals to kill them. However, if plants are weakened by lack of sunlight or anything else, their defenses are weakened. In that way, plants are much like people. When you are healthy, you are better able to fight germs. That's why doctors recommend getting enough rest, exercising, doing activities that are fun or relaxing, and eating fruits and vegetables! Of course, germs and pests still get the better of people—and plants, too!

How to Keep Away Tiny Pests

The same strong aromas and flavors we love about herbs seem to be a turnoff to pests. In fact, growing herbs beside your other plants may keep pests away. Vegetables, on the other hand, are a favorite of insects and other creepy crawlies. Here are four ways to keep them away.

1. For insects, spray the entire plant with a combination of 1 quart (0.9 L) water and 1–2 teaspoons (5–10 mL) dish soap or an organic pesticide.

2. For aphids, introduce predator insects, such as ladybugs.

3. Draw slugs away with potato slices. Early in the morning, collect the potato slices and throw them in the trash, where the slugs can live out the rest of their days.

4. Encourage predator animals in your garden, such as bats, birds, salamanders, frogs, snakes, and lizards. You can do this by providing water in the form of a small fountain or water garden, or by planting (or allowing to grow) native plants for shelter and additional food.

How to Avoid and Treat Disease

To avoid diseases, keep plants strong by watering enough but not too much, ensuring they are getting proper sunlight, and giving them plenty of space and nutrients. If a plant does get a disease, the diseased part should be discarded—not composted, lest the disease spread. Then, for a fungal disease, a fungicide can be applied—

purchased at the store or made naturally by mixing 1 tablespoon (15 mL) baking soda, 1 tablespoon (15 mL) vegetable oil, and a few drops of dish soap into 1 gallon of water. Spray the fungicide onto the plant using a spray bottle. For bacterial disease, remove the plant from the soil and replant in a pot (discarding the diseased parts). If an entire plant is diseased, discard it so that it doesn't spread to other plants. For more information, see plant descriptions.

One with the Wildlife

Aromatic flowers and tasty fruit and vegetables will beckon wildlife. You can build a cage, make a scarecrow, or blare talk radio (yes, really!) to scare animals away. Or you can make peace with them. Here are some ways to live and let live in the garden.

STRATEGY 1: PLENTY FOR EVERYONE

The simplest way to deal with wildlife is to plant enough to share. A squirrel is going to take an apple here and there. But two apple trees should produce so many apples that you won't miss the taken ones.

STRATEGY 2: DETER AND ATTRACT

Rodents don't like strong smells. Deter mice, squirrels, chipmunks, and bunnies by planting garlic or chives, or placing a pot of mint next to plants they are nibbling. Or sprinkle red pepper flakes at the base of their favorite plants. At the same time, attract them to another part of the garden with an open compost heap with lots of kitchen scraps.

STRATEGY 3: WELCOME PREDATORS

Why not let nature take care of itself? Attract carnivores to your garden, such as snakes, owls, hawks, bobcats, coyotes, and toads. (NOTE: Carnivores are dangerous to small pets, so consider this before rolling out the welcome mat!) Hunting makes carnivores thirsty, so provide a water source. Hiding spots allow them to go undetected. Add a pile of rocks for snakes, or a stack of wood for frogs and toads. To go the extra mile, create a habitat for predators—an owl box or toad hideout.

➢ a short, wide pot, water- and shade-loving plants, and a hollow log or small pot

Toads eat garden pests such as insects, slugs, and snails. They are attracted to shady, wet spots. Find a shady spot in the yard. Plant a short, wide pot with shade- and water-loving plants. Add a hollow log or a small pot turned on its side for shelter. Water daily.

I DID IT! DATE:

What Is Organic Gardening?

Organic gardeners grow plants without the use of synthetic fertilizer or pesticides. For organic gardeners, the focus is on building healthy soil by rotating crops and using organic matter, which not only fertilizes the plants but also feeds the living organisms in the soil so that they can support the plants in the long run. Organic gardeners also avoid seeds designated GMOs, genetically modified organisms. While all plants have been genetically altered, first by evolution, then by domestication and selective breeding, GMOs refer to organisms altered in a scientific laboratory.

Weeding

A weed is a plant that grows without being planted—or wanted. Weeds crowd other plants and hog the water and nutrients in the soil. Weeding should be done at least once a week. Pull them up from the root. Dig out stubborn roots with a fork or trowel.

Desirable "Weeds"

Note that not all plants that grow wild are weeds. It depends on if you want them there! Letting some native plants grow in your yard is a good way to attract wildlife and cultivate beauty with no cost and little work. However, even if you want some wild plants, you probably

DANDELION

don't want them everywhere. Trees in unwanted places should be dug up, roots and all. Fast-growing native vines should be cut back each year, lest they take over the whole yard. Even cheery dandelions (if that's your opinion of them) are ruthless nutrient thieves, so pull them up when they grow beside your cultivated plants.

Bad Weeds

On the other end of the spectrum, some weeds are more than pesky intruders. They're also harmful. Poison ivy, poison oak, and poison sumac produce an oil called urushiol that when touched causes an allergic reaction in most people in the form of an itchy rash that lasts for several days. People who are severely allergic may have complications requiring medical care. Know how to identify harmful weeds and avoid touching them. When addressing dangerous weeds, wear discardable clothing (such as a paper surgical gown) and gloves.

Tape the gloves to your sleeves. To avoid touching your face with the gloves, tie long hair back and have a clean stick handy for scratching. Pull up vines, and discard in the trash. They should not go in the compost pile. Do not burn them, as the fumes are dangerous. Finally, remove your discardable clothing without letting the outside touch your skin. Throw it away. Take a shower right away to remove any oils that got on you. Even taking precautions, you can still get a urushiol rash. Treat minor rashes with lotion designed to treat poison ivy. If the rash appears on more than one part of your body, is on your face or genitals, or is making it difficult to sleep, a doctor can prescribe steroid medication. Poison ivy will grow back. An adult can apply an herbicide to slow its growth.

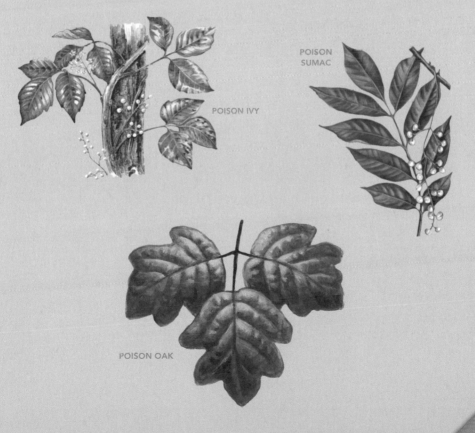

POISON SUMAC

POISON IVY

POISON OAK

TRACK IT ↘ Wild Plants and Animals

List the wild plants you have growing in your yard, the animals you've seen visiting them, and any plans you have (let it be, prune it, remove it, trellis it, etc.).

WILD PLANT NAME	WILD ANIMALS THAT VISIT

PLANS FOR THE PLANT

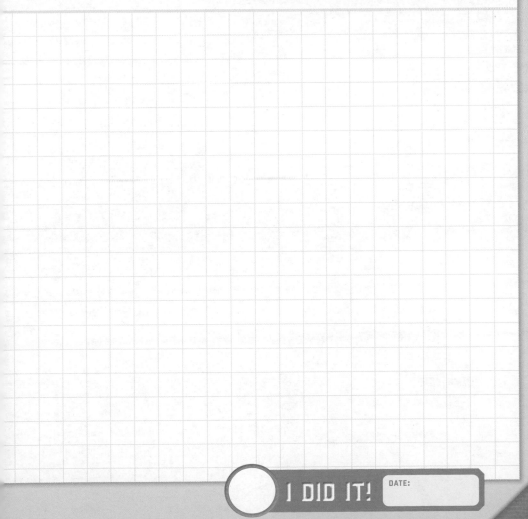

PART II

HERBS AND SPICES

J. DAWSON

What would YOU do?

Walking your dog, you spot a butterfly on a purple flower. You lean in to take a closer look and jump at the sound of a voice. "Rub the leaves and smell it!" your neighbor says from across the yard. You do this. It smells like . . . gum. She walks out with scissors and snips some of the branches. "Take some. It's mint. You can put it in your iced tea or make chocolate mint desserts with it. Just root them in water and then put them in a pot. They grow like weeds." Chocolate mint desserts sound amazing. But do you have room in your garden? And will this strategy really work? *What would you do?*

CHAPTER 1

Growing Herbs and Spices

Herbs and spices are plants grown for their strong flavors, aromas, or medicinal effects. For thousands of years people have used them to flavor food, cover bad smells, treat ailments, and solve household problems. As a food, what sets herbs and spices apart from fruit or vegetables is the strength of their flavor. With these plants, a little goes a long way.

Herbs and spices may be grown for their leaves, seeds, fruit, roots, bark, or some combination. The distinction between an herb and a spice is complicated. Sometimes, plants are differentiated by those grown for their leaves (herbs) and anything else (spices). There are exceptions. Chamomile flowers are considered an herb, for instance. Another distinction is that an herb is often used as a fresh plant whereas a spice is used dried. In this book, we try to follow these (loose) distinctions as closely as possible. Where spices are mentioned in this chapter, there is an asterisk.

CHAMOMILE

Herbs and spices can grow as annuals, perennials, shrubs, or trees. Spices tend to grow in consistently warm climates and be more difficult to grow. (Many spices grow on tropical trees, for instance.) Herbs, on the other hand, grow in various zones. They tend to be low-maintenance and pest-free. Many are heat- and drought-resistant. The strong aroma and taste deter

CLOVES

insects and other animals from nibbling them. There are exceptions: parsley, fennel, and dill are favorites of butterfly caterpillars, though you may not mind sharing your plants with such beautiful creatures.

Growing Tips for Herbs

Herbs are among the easiest plants to grow. They take up a small amount of space, need little water, and require only the nutrients added to the soil at the beginning of the season. Most annuals and perennials fit in a 5-gallon (19 L) pot or smaller, or a 12-inch (30.5 cm) square in the ground. The soil should be prepared by adding organic matter at the beginning of the season. Seeds and seedlings should be watered every few days if it is hot but can go a week in milder temperatures. Leaves can be harvested anytime, although, in some cases, they taste better before the plant flowers. Leaves should be pinched off at the top, along with a few inches of stem. This strengthens the plant and makes it grow fuller rather than tall and spindly. Flowers are usually harvested once they bloom. They can be plucked by hand or harvested with a flower rake. For seeds, pick the plant as late as possible but before the seeds fall to the ground. At the end of the season, pull up annuals but leave perennials in the ground or carry them inside if they are not cold-hardy. At the beginning of next season, pull off the dead or woody parts of the plant, or cut the plant back to about two inches above ground. This will allow for fresh growth. More specific information can be found in the herb descriptions.

Herbs and Spices: Where Did That Come From?

mint (leaves)

chamomile (flowers)

cloves (unopened dried flowers)

pepper (dried seed)

vanilla (seed)

ginger (root)

cinnamon (bark)

paprika (fruit)

First Aid Herbs

Beyond the pantry, some herbs are grown for their medicinal value. An aloe leaf can be broken and squeezed onto a burn. A lamb's ear leaf can be applied to a mild wound to stop bleeding.

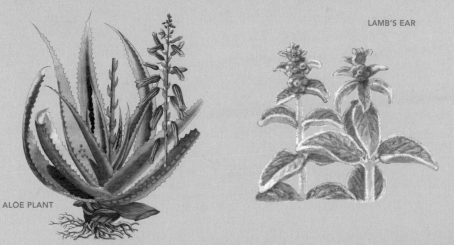

LAMB'S EAR

ALOE PLANT

Pet Herbs

Catnip and cat grass are delicious to cats. They can nibble them fresh or dry.

CATNIP

CAT GRASS

Deadly Herbs

Some herbs grown for their medicinal benefits are deadly except for (or even, in) the smallest quantities.

DEADLY NIGHTSHADE

Why it's dangerous: Deadly nightshade grows berries that are sweet at first but deadly in small amounts. Just two can kill a child, and ten, an adult. This plant is the number one reason that adults tell kids (rightly so) never to eat wild berries unless they know what they are.

Why it's an herb: Deadly nightshade, also known as Belladonna, was used as an anesthesia during surgery long ago.

FOXGLOVE

Why it's dangerous: Both the flowers and berries can cause heart failure.

Why it's an herb: Foxglove is used in small, regulated quantities as heart medicine because it makes the heart beat stronger.

CASTOR OIL PLANT

Why it's dangerous: The seeds are extremely poisonous, and sadly, there is no antidote.

Why it's an herb: Castor oil has been used for thousands of years and helps with a variety of common ailments ranging from acne to constipation. Surprisingly, castor oil comes from seeds that are deadly unless heated.

ERGOT

Why it's dangerous: Ergot is a fungus that disguises itself as part of the rye plant. It causes convulsions and hallucinations and may have been the cause of the behaviors displayed during the Salem witch trials.

Why it's an herb: It has historically been used as medicine in childbirth.

CHAPTER 2

Tea Herbs

Tea herbs may seem sophisticated, but they are simple to grow. Plant seeds or cuttings from an existing plant. Water during times of drought. Then enjoy them year after year! While any herb can be used to make tea—even traditional cooking herbs, such as rosemary, thyme, and basil—some are tried and true favorites. The beauty of herbs is they have a variety of uses. Tea herbs can also be tossed in a salad or made into a soothing eye pillow, heating pad, or bath sachet.

Chamomile

German chamomile is the quintessential herbal tea. It is made from the flowers of a chamomile plant. Chamomile seeds can be sown directly into your garden or grown in a pot and moved indoors for the winter. It is an annual, but because it self-seeds (drops seeds that sprout the following spring), it often returns year after year. Note that Roman chamomile is a perennial ground cover, the flowers of which can also be used in tea but are not very plentiful.

Grow Chamomile for Tea

> **WHAT YOU'LL NEED**
>
> ➤ German chamomile seeds, a pot, and potting mix or a garden bed

STEP 1 In a pot or garden bed, add a pinch of seeds every 8 inches (20.5 cm). Important: Chamomile needs sunlight to germinate, so seeds should be left atop the soil. Press them into the damp soil so that they don't blow away.

STEP 2 When plants sprout and grow two leaves, thin to 1 per 8 inches (20.5 cm).

STEP 3 Chamomile is ready to pick when the flowers bloom. Pinch off the flowers with your fingers or use a flower rake.

STEP 4 Throw the flowers into your teapot, 6–8 tsp (30–39 mL) per cup (236.5 mL) of water.

I DID IT! DATE:

Mint

MINT

Mint can be added to tea, eaten raw for its breath-freshening power, used as a garnish, or baked in desserts. You have several choices for mint varieties. Peppermint is the most potent, but spearmint is the most common. Then there is orange mint, chocolate mint, and lemon mint, which have hints of the flavors in their names.

Mint spreads by sending out new roots underground. Many plants do this, but mint is a bully in the garden, pushing out any plant in its way. For this reason, most gardeners grow mint in pots. In fact, mint is so easy to grow that simply breaking off a sprig of a neighbor's plant and plopping it in potting mix is often enough to grow a new plant. If you don't have access to a mint plant, buy seedlings rather than seeds. Later, you can share sprigs from your own plant. You can pick mint leaves at any time. Mint flowers also taste like mint and can be brewed for tea. Left alone, the flowers attract bees and butterflies.

Lemon Herbs

LEMONGRASS

Many herbs have a lemon flavor that's desirable in tea.

Lemon balm is a perennial that can be planted in the ground or in a pot so that it can be moved inside to use throughout the winter. Grow lemon balm in partial sun. It can be started from seed after all danger of frost, or indoors at any time.

From tropical Asia, lemongrass can survive winters in zones 8 and higher or can be grown in a pot and moved indoors in cooler climates. The stalks are used in cooking in the same way as green onions, but with a lemon flavor. Higher up on the stalks, the grass leaves can be clipped for tea. The leaves can also be dried.

The lemony-est of the lemon plants, lemon verbena smells like lemon drops. This sun- and heat-loving perennial can survive winters in zones 8 and higher or be moved indoors for the winter. Inside, it will drop its leaves. Move it outside in spring, and it will grow again.

LEMON VERBENA

More Tea-rrific Herbs

Rose hips are the fruit of the rose plant. If you allow a rose to wilt on the vine, the rose hip is what remains. Old-fashioned or wild roses, such as rugosa roses, produce the most rose hips. They can be used fresh or dry in tea.

ROSE HIPS

Cinnamon basil is basil with a cinnamon flavor. Pinch off leaves at the top to prevent flowering, at which point the plant weakens. An annual, it's best grown outdoors and used fresh.

CINNAMON BASIL

Among the prettiest and most fragrant of herbs, lavender can be grown in a pot, or in the ground, making a nice hedge for gardens and walkways. Lavender leaves and flowers can be used in tea or baked goods. Dried and mixed with rice, it also makes a soothing yoga eye pillow.

For a soothing, licorice-flavored tea, plant anise hyssop. This 3–5 foot (91–152 cm) tall flowering herb is often grown in perennial gardens. Both its leaves and flowers can be used in tea—or to flavor baked goods. The flowers are a favorite of bees and butterflies.

ANISE HYSSOP

5 Herbs to Grow from Seed

BORAGE The celery-flavored leaves can be added to soups and stews. Sow directly into the pot or garden bed—they do not like to be transplanted.

BORAGE

DILL

DILL Use it to make pickles or to flavor creamy sauces. Sow directly into the pot or garden bed—they do not like to be transplanted.

FENNEL The seeds deepen the flavor of sauces. Sow directly into the pot or garden bed—they do not like to be transplanted.

CHAMOMILE The tea herb is easy to grow and self-seeding.

FENNEL

PARSLEY Packed with vitamins, parsley can be added to warm or cold dishes, or eaten raw. It's slow to sprout, but the seeds can be helped along by soaking them in warm water for 24 hours before planting.

PARSLEY

CHAMOMILE

5 Herbs to Grow from Cuttings (or from Purchased Seedlings)

To grow a plant from a cutting, you can root it in water first, or dip the stem into rooting hormone—a liquid or powder than encourages roots to grow—before putting it in the potting mix. But often it will grow if you simply break a twig off at the branch and bury the bottom part of the stem one inch deep in potting mix or soil.

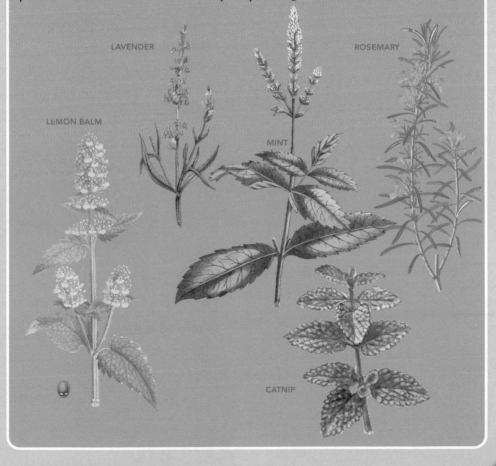

LAVENDER

ROSEMARY

LEMON BALM

MINT

CATNIP

WHAT YOU'LL NEED

➢ a 3–4 inch (7.5–10 cm) sprig of mint from a healthy plant, a plastic bottle, 1–15 gallon (4–57 L) pot, and potting mix

STEP 1 Fill the plastic bottle with water.

STEP 2 Place the stem only in the water. The narrow bottle top will prevent the leaves from getting wet, which can cause rot.

STEP 3 Change the water every other day.

STEP 4 When the roots are 0.5 inches (12.5 mm) long, plant the mint in a 1–15 gallon (4–57 L) pot. It will fill the whole pot over time.

STEP 5 Mint needs water only during periods of drought. The pot can be left outside for the winter or carried in for mint year-round.

STEP 6 To harvest, pinch off the tops of the mint sprigs. This will make the plant grow thicker and stronger.

I DID IT! DATE:

TRACK IT ⬎ Herbs I've Grown

List the herbs you've grown, and write whether you grew them from seed, seedling, or cutting. Note whether you used it in cooking, brewing tea, or first aid.

HERBS:	HOW I GREW THEM:	HOW I USED THEM:

I DID IT! DATE:

TAKE IT TO THE NEXT LEVEL ⬈

Dry Herbs Three Ways

For any of the three methods, choose a dry location (not the basement) and keep out of direct sunlight. When the herbs are completely dry, store the edible portions in sealed glass jars for up to one year.

OPTION 1 ▸ Lay a few sprigs in a basket to dry for three weeks.

OPTION 2 ▸ Tie 10–15 stems together and hang upside down for three weeks. If you are harvesting seeds, place a bowl or bag underneath.

OPTION 3 ▸ Spread several sprigs on a nylon or stainless-steel screen (not any other metal as it may rust), or a piece of paper, and allow to dry for three weeks.

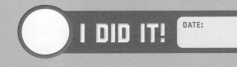

I DID IT! DATE:

CHAPTER 3

Cooking Herbs

Herbs can make any dish taste more complex and satisfying. But there are so many. Which should you grow? Starting out, you'll probably want low-maintenance herbs that will thrive in your grow zone or indoors. Beyond that, check the spice drawer for containers that are partially empty or recently replaced. Those are the herbs your family uses. They would surely appreciate some fresh versions of their favorite flavorings. You may also want to grow herbs that go with the vegetables you're growing. For further inspiration, consider growing some of the world's classic herb combinations.

Veggies + Herbs and Spices = Love

Tomato + basil + garlic = bruschetta

Tomato + onion + lime + cilantro = pico de gallo

Veggies + plain yogurt or sour cream + chives = veggies and dip

Cucumbers + dill + mustard + coriander = dill pickles

Classic Combos

Certain herb and spice combinations have become classics. Note that you don't have to grow the entire mixture in your garden. Substitute store-bought herbs for those that are too difficult or time-consuming to grow.

BLACKENING ▶

Made of paprika, garlic, thyme, oregano, and black pepper, white pepper, and cayenne pepper

PAPRIKA

THYME

GARLIC

OREGANO

BLACK PEPPER

WHITE PEPPER

CAYENNE PEPPER

Sprinkled on Cajun meat or fish dishes, the paprika turns reddish black during searing.

GARAM MASALA

It may include cinnamon, cardamom, nutmeg, mace, cloves, coriander, and cumin.

Traditional Indian curry dishes do not use Westernized curry powder (see below), but rather a spice combination that varies by region.

CORIANDER

CARDAMOM

CINNAMON   CUMIN   MACE   NUTMEG   CLOVES

CURRY POWDER

Made of turmeric, coriander, cumin, and ground ginger

Originating in England, this combination is meant to evoke the flavors of Indian cuisine. Note that there is also a curry plant that smells like curry powder but doesn't taste like it.

CUMIN

GINGER

CORIANDER

TUMERIC

FINES HERBES

Made of parsley, chives, tarragon, and chervil

In French cooking, three classic combinations are herbes de Provence, bouquet garni, and fines herbes, a delicate mix that is often added to omelets.

TARRAGON   CHERVIL   PARSLEY   CHIVES

FIVE-SPICE

Made of star anise, cinnamon, cloves, fennel seeds, Sichuan peppercorns

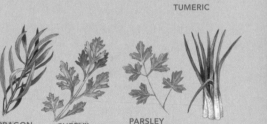
CINNAMON   FENNEL SEEDS

Common in Chinese cooking, five-spice brings out the five flavors detectable by our taste buds: sweet, sour, salty, bitter, and umami (the savory flavor of foods such as broth, mushrooms, and soy sauce).

CLOVES

SICHUAN PEPPERCORNS

STAR ANISE

ITALIAN

Made of oregano, thyme, marjoram, basil, rosemary

The seasoning labeled "Italian" in the store consists of five spices common in Italian cooking.

BASIL

ROSEMARY

MARJORAM

THYME

OREGANO

SCARBOROUGH FAIR

Made of parsley, sage, rosemary, and thyme

"Are you going to Scarborough Fair? Parsley, sage, rosemary, and thyme." Part ballad, part shopping list, this folk song features an herb combination that is easy to grow. Try stuffing it into a whole chicken or sprinkling over potatoes before roasting.

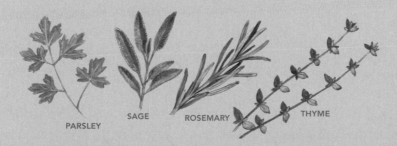

PARSLEY

SAGE

ROSEMARY

THYME

TRY IT → Grow a Vertical Herb Garden

A vertical garden is a garden that makes use of vertical space by having shelves, hanging plants, or stacked structures like this one.

The large pot should hold three herbs; the medium pot, two; and the small pot, one. Choose from one of the groups above, or create your own signature flavor combo!

> **WHAT YOU'LL NEED**
>
> ➢ 1 each: 15-gallon (56.5 L), 7-gallon (26.5 L), and 1-gallon (3.5 L) planters; outdoor paint (optional); and plastic bottles for filler

STEP 1 ▷ Paint the pots if you'd like.

STEP 2 ▷ Fill the large planter halfway and the medium planter one quarter way with plastic bottles to conserve potting mix.

STEP 3 ▷ Fill the largest pot with potting mix, leaving 2 inches (5 cm) at the top. If going on a deck or balcony, place it in a corner so that it has support.

STEP 4 ▷ Place the medium pot on top of the large one and fill it with potting mix, leaving 2 inches (5 cm) at the top.

STEP 5 ▷ Place the smallest pot on top of the stack, filling it in the same manner with potting mix.

STEP 6 ▷ Line up all the edges of the pots at the back so that you have the most space in the front of the large and medium pots.

STEP 7 Choose herbs to plant on each tier. The large pot will hold 3 small herb plants; the medium pot, 2; and the top pot, 1.

STEP 8 Create a signature blend of herbs from your garden. List the herbs in your signature blend and how you used it (in tea, cooking, baking, etc.).

My signature blend:

How I used it:

I DID IT! DATE:

TAKE IT TO THE **NEXT LEVEL** ↗

Make Herbed Root Vegetables

STEP 1 Preheat the oven to 425°F (218°C).

STEP 2 Choose your favorite root vegetables, such as potatoes, carrots, turnips, or radish.

STEP 3 Chop them into 1-inch (2.5 cm) pieces so that they make 4 cups (946 mL).

STEP 4 Melt 0.5 cup (118 mL) of butter. (Or substitute olive oil for a vegan option.) Add to it 3 T (44 mL) of fresh chopped herbs from your signature blend, or 1 T (15 mL) dry.

STEP 5 Pour over the veggies and roast for 20 minutes.

I DID IT! DATE:

Garlic and Other Bulbs

Chives, green onions, shallots, leeks, garlic, and onions are alliums. They are members of the lily family. Allow a garlic plant to flower and you will see the resemblance! Those with smaller bulbs are considered herbs, whereas onions are generally thought of as vegetables, perhaps because of their size or the quantity called for in recipes. Alliums grow from a clove or bulb, which sometimes spreads underground to form more cloves or bulbs. They are sun lovers and need only be watered during droughts.

Chives are the most cost-effective of the alliums. Plant them once, and they will return and multiply each year—producing edible roots, stems, and flowers. You can start them as seeds indoors and then transplant them into your garden, spaced 12 inches (30.5 cm) apart.

Garlic grows by multiplying its cloves. Pull apart the cloves of fresh garlic from the grocery store and plant each, 6 inches (15 cm) apart, in the fall. By midsummer, each clove will have multiplied into several. In the meantime, a curly green stem with a lily-like flower will have grown. These can be clipped, chopped, and sauteed or eaten as a raw topping like green onions. Later, the garlic bulb is ready to be harvested when the rest of the stem and leaves yellow—about midway through the summer.

Shallots, rather than onions, are often called for in gourmet recipes, and they are expensive to buy. However, they are inexpensive and easy to grow. Plant shallot "sets"—small shallots—in a pot, or a plot, 6 inches apart in the fall and spring, and they will multiply and be ready throughout the summer as their tops yellow.

SHALLOT

TRY IT → Grow Garlic

➣ a garlic bulb from the store, a 60-inch (152 cm) row in the garden or a large pot, and a trowel or spoon

STEP 1 In the fall before the ground freezes, prepare a spot in the garden. Each garlic bulb typically contains 10 cloves, which should be spaced every 6 inches (15 cm).

STEP 2 Pull apart the garlic, clove by clove. Plant the cloves pointy side up every 6 inches (15 cm). Press them 1–2 inches (2.5–5 cm) deep into the soil.

STEP 3 In the spring, once the flower buds, the curly part of the stem and the bud can be harvested, peeled, and used for garlic flavor in cooking.

STEP 4 Later, when the rest of the stem and leaves turn yellow, dig up the new garlic bulbs. Brush off loose dirt and allow the garlic to dry. Don't let them get wet!

STEP 5 After 2–3 weeks, the rest of the dirt can be brushed off, and the garlic is ready to eat. You can save some of the larger cloves to plant next year!

I DID IT! DATE:

CHAPTER 4

Spices

A spice is a flavoring that comes from a part of the plant other than the leaves, especially the seed, fruit, or bark. It gets tricky because some flowers (chamomile) are considered herbs and others (cloves) are considered spices. And sometimes the terms are used interchangeably. Spices tend to be more labor-intensive to grow than leafy herbs. Leaves are the most plentiful and readily available parts of a plant, whereas seeds and flowers are smaller and more difficult to accumulate in large quantities, and roots and bark are less readily accessible. In addition, many spices grow on tropical plants unsuited for North American climates. For these reasons, spices are not as popular as herbs among home growers. However, some are not as difficult to grow as you might think. And others might be just the challenge you are seeking!

Seeds, Flowers, and Fruit

Seeds, flowers, and fruit are all related to the plant's reproductive system. Most plants produce flowers, though not necessarily showy bouquet flowers. Flowers grow on the tips of long grass, at the tops of trees, and on vegetable plants (broccoli is a flower). Each flower contains a male stamen and female carpel, which includes the style and ovary. Pollen from the male stamen travels to the female style (often carried by butterflies, bees, and birds). It travels down the style to the ovary. Inside, ovules in the ovary become seeds, and the rest of the ovary becomes the fruit protecting the seeds. When the fruit forms, the flower wilts and dies. Eventually the fruit bursts open or is eaten, and the seed is dispersed. If it lands in an ideal spot, it grows into a new plant. Or, somewhere along the line, you may gather the flower, fruit, or seeds and eat them.

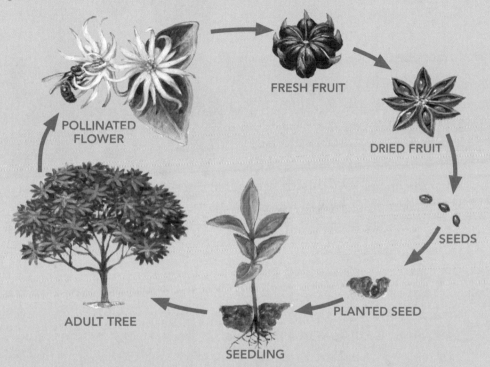

POLLINATED FLOWER

FRESH FRUIT

DRIED FRUIT

SEEDS

PLANTED SEED

SEEDLING

ADULT TREE

Gather flower spices before or soon after they bloom. Cloves are the dried flower buds of the clove tree. Whole cloves are too tough to eat but can be simmered in cider (easiest method is to press the cloves into an orange so that you don't have to fish out loose cloves). Cloves are also ground and used like cinnamon. Clove trees are tall evergreens that grow in the tropics. They can be grown indoors, but it takes several years for the flowers to grow.

Gather fruit spices when the flower has wilted. Star anise is the dry fruit of the Chinese star anise tree, which is native to China and Vietnam. It prefers a warm, wet environment. Native to southwest

India, cardamom plants yield the fruit known as cardamom. The sweet spice is common in Indian, Middle Eastern, and Swedish dishes, and in teas and coffees. It can be grown as a houseplant or outdoors in warm grow zones, but a single plant will not produce many fruits—and will only do so after about three years. Black pepper is the berry of the black pepper vine, a native of south India. It grows up trees in the forest understory and so does well as a houseplant in the

BLACK PEPPER

dappled light of indoors. The berries can be picked and dried when they are green for cracked pepper.

Harvest seed spices when the fruit has ripened or dried on the vine. Sweet fennel is a licorice-flavored plant used for both its leaves and seeds. A not-so-hardy perennial, it dies in freezing temperatures but may self-seed and grow back the next year. Cumin, a smoky-flavored spice found in curry dishes, is another warm-weather annual. It can be started indoors in a pot and carried outside for the summer.

In contrast, mustard greens are cool-weather plants. As the name suggests, they are more popularly grown in gardens for their greens than seeds. But, allowed to flower, mustard will produce seeds in pods. Native to the tropics of Mexico, vanilla is a vining plant, the pods of which are harvested for the seeds and essential oils. It's hard to grow, but you can try planting it inside in partial sun with support for vining. To produce fruit, the plant will need to be hand-pollinated with a toothpick.

Peppercorn plants are grown in the tropics of India and Sri Lanka. The ideal grow zone is 12, but they may be able to survive in zones 10 and 11. They can also be grown inside if the temperature remains above 65°F (18°C).

WHAT YOU'LL NEED

➤ small peppercorn plant, 5-gallon (19 L) or larger container, trowel or spoon, trellis, potting mix, and a fertilizer that is equal parts nitrogen, phosphorus, and potassium

STEP 1 Purchase a small pepporoorn plant from a nursery.

STEP 2 Plant it in a 5-gallon (19 L) or larger container. Attach a trellis on which the vine can grow. Place it in a sunny window in a warm room.

STEP 3 Water the plant whenever tho top of the potting mix becomes dry.

STEP 4 Every 2 weeks, add a fertilizer that is equal parts nitrogen, phosphorus, and potassium. Do this by mixing the fertilizer into water as directed, and then watering the plant.

STEP 5 When the outdoor temperature is unlikely to drop below 60°F (16°C), move the plant outside into dappled sunlight.

STEP 6 Gather the peppercorns when they are green. Allow them to dry until they are black. Now you can put them in a pepper mill to use as seasoning.

I DID IT! DATE:

TRY IT → Harvest Seeds

WHAT YOU'LL NEED

➢ scissors or snips, sheet of paper, paper bag, and a jar with a secure lid

STEP 1 To harvest seeds, first make sure they are fully mature.

STEP 2 Clip the seedy parts of the plant, along with several inches of the stem.

STEP 3 Dry the seedy plant on a sheet of paper or hang it by its stem over the paper bag.

STEP 4 When the seeds are dry, shake them into the bag, freeing them from the rest of the plant. Remove the seeds from the bag and return them to the paper to dry for 2 more weeks.

STEP 5 When they are fully dry, store them in an airtight jar. If you let the seeds of annuals fall to the ground, they may grow the next year.

I DID IT! DATE:

Roots, Rhizomes, and Bark

A root is a part of the plant that anchors it to the ground and absorbs water and nutrients. Roots usually grow underground, but not everything that grows underground is a root. A rhizome is a stem that grows horizontally underground. Spices grown for their roots and rhizomes are typically dug up to slice off a piece and then reburied in the soil. Cousins ginger and turmeric are the most famous of the rhizome spices. Both grow as 3-foot (91 cm) tall, warm-weather plants. Turmeric is a main ingredient in curry powder and is what makes mustard sauce bright yellow. Ginger is used in Asian cooking and sweets such as gingersnaps. Both have an earthy flavor popular in fall coffees and teas, and creamy dishes, because fats found in coconut milk and butter mellow the bitter flavor. Fresh rhizomes may be available in garden stores or the grocery store.

GINGER

Marshmallow is a plant grown for its roots—and other parts, too. Native to America, you can find it growing in wetlands, hence the name. If you keep the soil moist, you can grow marshmallow as a perennial in zones 3–9. It's no coincidence that there is a candy with the same name. Marshmallows were originally made by boiling marshmallow root. This made a gelatinous mixture that was then whipped with sugar and allowed to cool. Nowadays, store-bought gelatin takes the place of the marshmallow root—but you can still try making this candy the old-fashioned way.

Cinnamon is a unique spice in that it comes from the bark of various related trees—most of which grow in Sri Lanka. First the outer bark is removed from the tree and then the inner bark. When the inner bark dries, it forms the quills that are called cinnamon sticks. They are ground into cinnamon. You can grow a cinnamon tree outdoors in zones 10–11, or in a pot elsewhere. Getting to the inner bark is labor-intensive, but you can enjoy the cinnamon smell of the inedible fruit. Less enjoyable is the flower, which smells rotten.

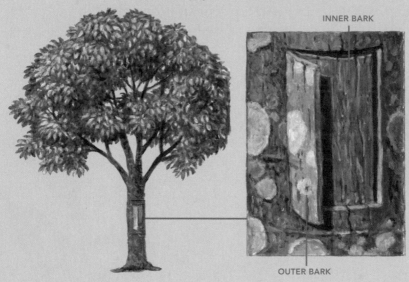

INNER BARK

OUTER BARK

Pumpkin Pie Spices

Pumpkin pie spices have a similar taste, but they come from different sources.

NUTMEG

NUTMEG the seed of the nutmeg tree

ALLSPICE the berry of the *Pimenta dioica* tree

CINNAMON bark of a cinnamon tree

GINGER rhizome of a ginger plant

Grow Ginger in a Pot

Choose ginger rhizomes that have sprout-y eyes like those on potatoes. Organic ginger is your best bet, as other ginger may have been treated to prevent sprouting.

> **WHAT YOU'LL NEED**
> ➢ ginger rhizomes, 3-inch pot, potting mix, trowel or spoon, ziplock bag, and larger pots for potting up

STEP 1 Place a root piece with an eye pointing up in a 3-inch pot, 1 inch deep.

STEP 2 Water the potting mix so that it is damp but not soaking.

STEP 3 Put the whole thing in a ziplock bag and keep at 70°F (21°C). The sprout will emerge in 6–8 weeks. Pot up as the plant grows. Ginger thrives at 60–90°F (16–32°C). If the roots peak out of the potting mix as they grow, cover them with more potting mix.

STEP 4 After a few months, harvest some of the ginger by pulling up the plant by its stem and snapping off a piece. Then set the plant back into the pot to keep growing.

I DID IT! DATE:

HERB GUIDE

Herbs are among the easiest plants to grow. Whether planted in pots or in the ground, they grow quickly and require minimal care. Spices tend to be more labor-intensive, but if you're up for a challenge, go for it!

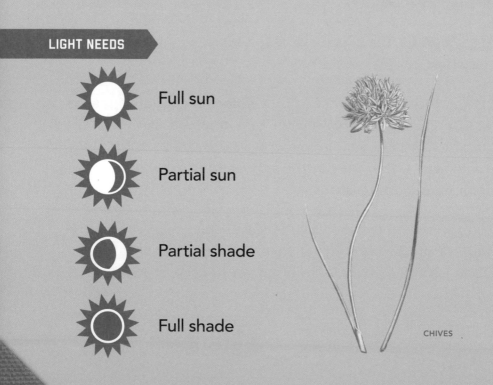

Full sun

Partial sun

Partial shade

Full shade

CHIVES

BASIL

CHEVRIL

BAY LAUREL
(WITH FLOWERS)

Aloe Vera
(Aloe barbadensis)

DESCRIPTION 2–3 foot (61–91 cm) tall succulent with leaves containing gel that can be used to treat minor sunburns, burns, and wounds
NOTE: Some people are allergic to aloe and will have a reaction to its use on skin. Aloe should not be eaten.

HARDY ZONES 10–11, or indoors

PLANT Plant a young plant or offset in well-draining soil or potting mix to cover the root. A terra-cotta pot is best.

SPACE 24 inches (61 cm) in ground or a 5-gallon (19 L) pot

CARE Water your aloe plant every 3 weeks. Remove pups that grow beside it. These can be planted in a separate pot.

HARVEST To treat a wound, remove a leaf, break, and squeeze out the gel.

DISEASES/PESTS Aloe is an easygoing plant. Root rot can be avoided by not overwatering.

VARIETIES/CULTIVARS tiger, lace, blue

POINT OF FACT Aloe vera has been valued for its medical properties for more than 2,000 years and was transported along the ancient Silk Road.

I GREW IT!

WHEN I GREW IT
DATE

NOTES

Anise Hyssop
(Agastache foeniculum)

to

DESCRIPTION 2–4 foot (61–122 cm) tall plant with leaves and flowers that taste like anise (a different herb). The flowers also attract bees and butterflies.

HARDY ZONES 4–8

PLANT Plant seeds 2 weeks after the last frost date. Sow seeds every few inches in an even line or a few seeds in a 5-gallon (19 L) pot. Press into the soil or potting mix. The seeds need sunlight to germinate, so do not bury them.

SPACE 12 inches (30.5 cm)

CARE Water lightly.

HARVEST Harvest leaves in 30 days, flowers the second year.

DISEASES/PESTS Pests will leave anise hyssop alone.

VARIETIES/CULTIVARS alba, golden jubilee, licorice blue

POINT OF FACT Not to be confused with the spice star anise, anise hyssop is native to American prairies. Historically, it's been used to treat poison ivy and broken hearts.

I GREW IT!

WHEN I GREW IT
DATE

NOTES

Basil

(Ocimum basilicum)

DESCRIPTION 1.5–2 foot (46–61 cm) tall plant with fragrant and flavorful leaves

HARDY ZONES 2–11

PLANT Plant seeds in a pot indoors and move outside 2 weeks after the last frost date, or plant seedlings 2 weeks after the last frost date. Alternately, you can root a cutting and plant that.

SPACE 12 inches (30.5 cm)

CARE Water moderately. Basil will naturally reach the end of its life span when it flowers. You can grow basil year-round by rooting a cutting before the end of the season and planting it inside.

HARVEST Harvest leaves in 60–90 days. Pinch off the tops of the plant to harvest the leaves. This will prevent it from flowering.

DISEASES/PESTS Japanese beetles can be picked off by hand; aphids can be controlled with ladybugs.

VARIETIES/CULTIVARS African blue, cinnamon, lemonette

POINT OF FACT Basil is the main ingredient in dishes such as pesto.

I GREW IT!

WHEN I GREW IT

DATE

NOTES

TREE
Bay Laurel
(Laurus nobilis)

DESCRIPTION 8-foot (2.5 m) or taller evergreen tree with fragrant and flavorful leaves. Whole leaves are added to dishes and removed before eating.

HARDY ZONES 8–10, or indoors

PLANT Plant a sapling in a 15-gallon (56.5 L) pot and set outdoors in warm weather. Bring inside when the temperature dips below 50°F (10°C).

SPACE 8 feet (2.5 m)

CARE Water moderately.

HARVEST Leaves for cooking can be harvested from the young tree.

DISEASES/PESTS Pests typically leave this plant alone.

POINT OF FACT Laurel wreaths were given to victors of the ancient Olympics. To "rest on your laurels" means to rely on past success rather than continuing to work.

I GREW IT!

WHEN I GREW IT
DATE

NOTES

....

Beach Rose
(Rosa rugosa)

to

DESCRIPTION A hardy shrub, 4–6 feet (1–2 m) tall and wide, with flowers that develop into fruit (hips)

HARDY ZONES 3–9

PLANT Plant saplings in the spring.

SPACE At least 3 feet (91 cm)

CARE Water heavily the first year and then lightly. Prune to control the shrub's sprawl.

HARVEST Harvest rose hips after the flowers have wilted.

DISEASES/PESTS The plant is hardy and disease-resistant.

VARIETIES/CULTIVARS Hansa, purple pavement, Frau Dagmar Hastrup

POINT OF FACT During World War II many countries used rose hips to provide necessary vitamin C to children. *Rugosa* means "wrinkled" in Latin and refers to the wrinkled leaves the shrub produces.

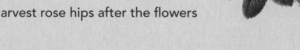

◖ I GREW IT!

WHEN I GREW IT
DATE

NOTES

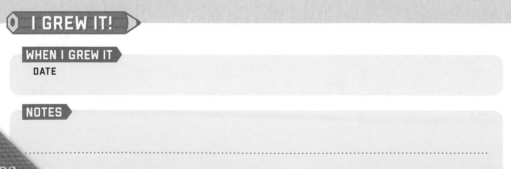

Black Pepper

(Piper nigrum)

DESCRIPTION 13-foot (4 m) vine with berries that can be dried and ground into a spice

HARDY ZONES 12, or indoors

PLANT Plant a young plant in a 5-gallon (19 L) terra-cotta container with a trellis, or in a hanging basket.

SPACE 12 inches (30.5 cm)

CARE Water lightly.

HARVEST The plant will flower in 3–4 years and produce fruit the following year. Harvest the berries when they are still green, and then dry. Grind them into black pepper.

DISEASES/PESTS Pests are rare. Disease can be avoided by keeping the plant warm. It should never be exposed to temperatures below 60°F (16°C) at night or 70°F (21°C) during the day. Note: Black spots on leaves are normal and not a sign of disease.

VARIETIES/CULTIVARS Malabar, sarawak, talamanca

POINT OF FACT Pepper was traded along the ancient Silk Road. Studies show that pepper helps the body absorb helpful nutrients.

 **I GREW IT!**

WHEN I GREW IT
DATE

NOTES

Borage
(Borago officinalis)

DESCRIPTION 1.5–2 foot (46–61 cm) tall plant with cucumber-flavored stems, leaves, and flowers

HARDY ZONES 2–11

PLANT Plant seeds 2 weeks after the last frost date. Sow seeds every few inches in an even line.

SPACE 12 inches (30.5 cm)

CARE Water weekly.

HARVEST Harvest leaves and flowers in 50–80 days. If you leave some of the flowers on the stems, they will self-seed and grow again next spring.

DISEASES/PESTS Borage is mostly disease- and pest-free.

VARIETIES/CULTIVARS Alba, common, creeping

POINT OF FACT Borage was used in medieval Europe to treat stomachaches, sore throats, and mental illness.

I GREW IT!

WHEN I GREW IT
DATE

NOTES

Cardamom
(Elettaria cardamomum)

DESCRIPTION 6–15 foot (1.5–4.5 m) tall tropical plant with fuzzy or slightly hairy leaves and fragrant, flavorful seedpods used to flavor food and drinks

HARDY ZONES 10–12

PLANT Plant a seedling in a 5–15 gallon (19–57 L) pot.

SPACE If planting in-ground, space 2–4 feet (61–122 cm apart)

CARE Water moderately.

HARVEST Harvest any seedpods before they are ripe, and then allow to sun-dry.

DISEASES/PESTS None known.

POINT OF FACT Many of the so-called cardamom plants sold in America are false cardamom, or *Alpinia nutans*, which has glossy rather than fuzzy leaves, and that smell like cardamom. Native to India, cardamom is also a staple of Scandinavian cooking. It is said to have been introduced by the Vikings.

I GREW IT!

WHEN I GREW IT
DATE

NOTES

PERENNIAL
Catnip
(Nepeta cataria)

DESCRIPTION 2-foot (61 cm) tall plant with leaves that cats like to eat

HARDY ZONES 3–7

PLANT Plant seeds 2 weeks after the last frost date. Sow seeds in an even line, every few inches.

SPACE 12 inches (30.5 cm)

HARVEST Harvest leaves in 12–15 weeks.

DISEASES/PESTS None known.

POINT OF FACT Catnip releases a chemical into the air that serves as an insect repellent. The same chemical causes cats to feel euphoric. This doesn't hurt the cats. (Note: Catnip can make dogs—and people—drowsy.) Housecats aren't the only ones to like catnip—so do lions and jaguars.

I GREW IT!

WHEN I GREW IT
DATE

NOTES

Cayenne Pepper
(Capsicum frutescens)

DESCRIPTION 1–3 foot (30.5–91 cm) tall plant bearing spicy fruit that can be eaten fresh or dried

HARDY ZONES 9–11, as an annual during the summer in zones 4–11, or indoors

PLANT Plant seedlings in the ground 2 weeks after the last frost date or seeds in a 2-gallon (7.5 L) pot.

SPACE 24 inches (61 cm)

CARE If grown in a pot, move indoors when the temperature drops below 60°F (16°C). Water moderately.

HARVEST Harvest peppers in 60–90 days.

DISEASES/PESTS Pick off snails and slugs. If aphids appear, spray the leaves with water.

VARIETIES/CULTIVARS Cowhorn, Carolina, ring of fire

POINT OF FACT Peppers are rated on the Scoville Heat Unit scale of 0–16,000,000 (pure capsaicin—the chemicals that make peppers hot). Cayenne peppers are rated 30,000–50,000—hotter than a jalapeño but milder than a habanero.

I GREW IT!

WHEN I GREW IT
DATE

NOTES

ANNUAL

Chamomile
(Matricaria recutita)

DESCRIPTION 2-foot (61 cm) tall plant with fragrant and flavorful flowers

HARDY ZONES 3–9

PLANT Plant seeds 4 weeks before the last frost date. Sow seeds every few inches.

SPACE 12 inches (30.5 cm)

CARE Water moderately.

HARVEST Harvest flowers in 60 days. (Note: If you leave some flowers on the stem so that seeds fall, chamomile will grow again next spring.)

DISEASES/PESTS Typical plant diseases can be avoided by not watering too much; pests such as aphids and caterpillars can be picked off.

POINT OF FACT In Greek, *chamomile* means "on the ground apple." The flowers smell faintly like apples. Chamomile tea has been drunk since ancient times.

I GREW IT!

WHEN I GREW IT

DATE

NOTES

Chervil
(Anthriscus cerefolium)

 to

DESCRIPTION 1–2 foot (30.5–61 cm) tall plant with flavorful leaves

HARDY ZONES 2–10

PLANT Plant seeds 2 weeks before the last frost date, or 2 weeks before the first frost date. Sow seeds every few inches in an even line, or in a 5 gallon (19 L) pot. Press into the soil. Cover with very little soil, if at all.

SPACE 12 inches (30.5 cm)

CARE Water moderately.

HARVEST Harvest leaves in 6–8 weeks.

DISEASES/PESTS None known.

VARIETIES/CULTIVARS Vertisimo, fine curled

POINT OF FACT Also known as French parsley, chervil is one of the fines herbes. The flavor of chervil has been described as a combination of tarragon, basil, and anise.

 **I GREW IT!**

WHEN I GREW IT
DATE

NOTES

....

Chives
(Allium schoenoprasum)

DESCRIPTION 1-foot (30.5 cm) tall plant with fragrant and flavorful bulbs, stems, and flowers

HARDY ZONES 3–12

PLANT Plant seeds 2 weeks after the last frost date, or in a 5 gallon (19 L) pot. Sow seeds every few inches in an even line.

SPACE 12 inches (30.5 cm)

CARE Water moderately. Chives multiply through their roots. Every few years, dig up chives and divide them. Bring chives indoors for year-round growth, or allow to go dormant in winter.

HARVEST Harvest stems and flowers in 60 days. Cut with scissors.

DISEASES/PESTS Spray off aphids.

VARIETIES/CULTIVARS Forescate, Corsican white, albiflorum

POINT OF FACT Chives grow wild and are recognizable by their purple flowers and onion smell.

I GREW IT!

WHEN I GREW IT
DATE

NOTES

ANNUAL

Cilantro/Coriander
(Coriandrum sativum)

DESCRIPTION 2-foot (61 cm) tall plant with fragrant and flavorful leaves and seeds. The leaves (cilantro) are used as an herb and its seeds (coriander) as a spice.

HARDY ZONES 3–11

PLANT Plant seeds 2 weeks after the last frost date in an even line every few inches; thin to 12 inches (30.5 cm) apart.

SPACE 12 inches (30.5 cm)

CARE Water moderately.

HARVEST Harvest leaves in 30 days, seeds in 90 days. (Note: Once the plant flowers and seeds, the leaves become too bitter to eat.) If you allow some of the seeds to fall, cilantro will grow again next spring.

DISEASES/PESTS Typical plant diseases can be avoided by not watering too much; pests such as aphids and caterpillars can be removed by pruning the plant.

POINT OF FACT Some people think cilantro smells and tastes like soap, a perception that scientists think is caused by a set of genetic variations.

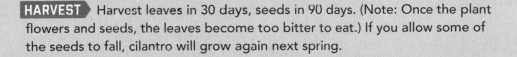

I GREW IT!

WHEN I GREW IT
DATE

NOTES

Cinnamon

(Cinnamomum zeylanicum or *Cinnamomum verum)*

DESCRIPTION 8–50 foot (2.5–15 m) tall tropical tree grown for its flavorful inner bark

HARDY ZONES 10–11, or indoors

PLANT Plant a young tree in a 25 gallon (95 L) container indoors or, in warm climates, outside in the ground. In a pot, use African violet potting mix.

SPACE 10 feet (3 m)

INNER BARK

OUTER BARK

CARE Water moderately. Fertilize every other week by adding organic matter such as fish emulsion to the water. Take a break from fertilizing in the winter. Mist the tree if the indoor air is dry.

HARVEST After 2 years, you can harvest branches that are 2 inches (5 cm) in diameter or wider. Break or saw off twigs and leaves. Use a knife to scrape off the outer bark. The cinnamon is the next layer. It's lighter than the outer bark but darker than the innermost layer. Use a knife to cut a gash just through the cinnamon layer. Now use your fingers to peel off the cinnamon layer. Put it in the sun to dry. It will curl up into cinnamon sticks.

DISEASES/PESTS If mealy bugs attack, the tree can be treated with neem-oil.

POINT OF FACT Cinnamon was used for embalming in ancient Egypt.

I GREW IT!

WHEN I GREW IT
DATE

NOTES

TREE

Cloves
(Syzygium aromaticum)

DESCRIPTION 8–40 foot (2.5–12 m) tall tree with fragrant and flavorful flower buds used as a spice

HARDY ZONES 12–13, or indoors

PLANT Plant seeds in a large pot filled with orchid potting mix. Keep damp until the seeds sprout. When they are a few inches tall, thin to one plant.

SPACE 10 feet (3 m)

CARE Water moderately. Spritz with water when the air is dry. The tree can be brought outside as long as the temperature does not drop below 60°F (16°C). Add organic fertilizer every year.

HARVEST Harvest a small number of flower buds in 6 years. The tree will produce a large number of cloves beginning its 20th year. Pick buds before they bloom and dry them in the sun.

DISEASES/PESTS Outside, check for bugs under leaves. Spray them off with water.

POINT OF FACT Clove is an ingredient in both Worcestershire sauce and ketchup. You can make a pomander, an aromatic decoration, by pressing cloves into oranges and allowing the orange to air-dry.

I GREW IT!

WHEN I GREW IT
DATE

NOTES

Cumin
(Cuminum cyminum)

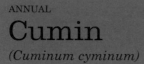

DESCRIPTION 1-foot (30.5 cm) tall plant with fragrant and flavorful foliage and seeds. The seeds are used to make cumin powder, a popular spice and ingredient in curry.

HARDY ZONES 5–10, or indoors

PLANT Plant seeds 2 weeks after the last frost date every few inches in a line, or in a 5 gallon (19 L) pot.

SPACE 12 inches (30.5 cm)

CARE Water moderately until established, and then lightly.

HARVEST Harvest seeds in 120 days. Cut the stems and hang over a bag to catch the seeds.

DISEASES/PESTS Prune parts of the plant affected by aphids and caterpillars.

POINT OF FACT The word *cumin* can be traced to the ancient Sumerian word *gamun.*

I GREW IT!

WHEN I GREW IT
DATE

NOTES

Dill
(Anethum graveolens)

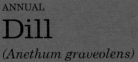

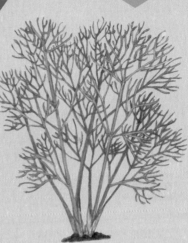

DESCRIPTION 2–4 foot (61–122 cm) tall plant with fragrant and flavorful foliage and seeds

HARDY ZONES All

PLANT Plant seeds 2 weeks after the last frost date. Sow seeds every few inches in an even line.

SPACE 12 inches (30.5 cm)

CARE Water moderately.

HARVEST Harvest leaves in 70 days, seeds in 90 days. If you allow some of the seeds to fall, dill will grow again next spring.

DISEASES/PESTS Swallowtail caterpillars can be removed by hand.

VARIETIES/CULTIVARS Hera, bouquet, fernleaf

POINT OF FACT Dill comes from the old Norse word *dylle*, to soothe or lull. It is believed to calm upset stomachs. Dill is an ingredient in tzatziki sauce.

I GREW IT!

WHEN I GREW IT
DATE

NOTES

PERENNIAL
Fennel
(Foeniculum vulgare)

DESCRIPTION 4–6 foot (1-1.5 m) tall plant with fragrant and flavorful foliage

HARDY ZONES 4–9

PLANT Plant seeds every few inches in the spring; thin once they sprout.

SPACE 3 feet (91 cm) when mature

CARE Water moderately.

HARVEST Harvest stems and leaves once the plant is established, fennel seeds after the plants flower.

DISEASES/PESTS Pick off swallowtail butterfly caterpillars by hand, if you have the heart.

POINT OF FACT Fennel is a popular vegetable in the Mediterranean region, and the seeds are a key ingredient in Italian sausage.

I GREW IT!

WHEN I GREW IT
DATE

NOTES

Garlic
(Allium sativum)

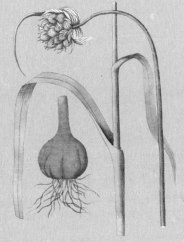

DESCRIPTION 1-foot (30.5 cm) tall plant grown for its fragrant and flavorful bulb

HARDY ZONES 5–9

PLANT Plant cloves in fall or early spring, 2 inches (5 cm) deep and 6 inches (15 cm) apart, pointy side up.

SPACE 6 inches (15 cm)

CARE Water moderately.

HARVEST Harvest flower buds before they bloom, bulbs when the stem and leaves yellow and fall over (late summer). Allow them to dry in the sun.

DISEASES/PESTS Garlic is usually disease- and pest-free.

VARIETIES/CULTIVARS Silverskin, artichoke, porcelain

POINT OF FACT In folklore, garlic repels vampires. In cooking, garlic kills harmful bacteria.

I GREW IT!

WHEN I GREW IT
DATE

NOTES

....

Ginger
(Zingiber officinale)

DESCRIPTION 2–4 foot (61–122 cm) tall and wide plant grown for its flavorful rhizomes

HARDY ZONES 9–11, or indoors

PLANT Plant 2-inch (5 cm) pieces of budding rhizomes just beneath the soil or in a pot.

SPACE 1–4 feet (30.5–122 cm)

CARE Water moderately. Bring indoors when temperatures drop below 50°F (10°C). Pot up every year or so.

HARVEST Harvest after several months by digging up the plant, snapping off a piece of rhizome, and replanting.

DISEASES/PESTS Avoid root rot by not letting the plant get too cold or wet.

POINT OF FACT The world's largest gingerbread house was built in Bryant, Texas. It was the size of a 5-bedroom house.

I GREW IT!

WHEN I GREW IT
DATE

NOTES

Lavender
(Lavandula)

DESCRIPTION A genus of plants 2–3 feet (61–91 cm) tall with fragrant and flavorful foliage and flowers

HARDY ZONES 5–8

PLANT Plant seeds or seedlings in the spring.

SPACE 2 feet (61 cm)

CARE Water lightly.

HARVEST Harvest flowers and leaves anytime.

DISEASES/PESTS Root rot is a problem during very cold (0°F/-18°C) or wet winters.

VARIETIES/CULTIVARS Thumbelina Leigh, buena vista, grosso

POINT OF FACT Provence, France, is known for its sprawling lavender fields.

I GREW IT!

WHEN I GREW IT
DATE

NOTES

PERENNIAL

Lemon Balm

(Melissa officinalis)

DESCRIPTION 1–2 foot (30.5–61 cm) tall plant grown for its lemony leaves

HARDY ZONES 3–7

PLANT Plant seeds or seedlings in the spring.

SPACE 2–3 feet (61–91 cm)

CARE Water lightly.

HARVEST Harvest leaves anytime.

DISEASES/PESTS Lemon balm is disease- and pest-free.

VARIETIES/CULTIVARS Compacta, aurea

POINT OF FACT Lemon balm is also called bee balm because bees love its flowers. Though a member of the mint family, lemon balm doesn't spread so aggressively.

I GREW IT!

WHEN I GREW IT
DATE

NOTES

PERENNIAL

Lemon Verbena

(Aloysia citrodora)

DESCRIPTION 3–6 foot (91–183 cm) tall and wide flowering plant with lemon-flavored leaves

HARDY ZONES 9–10, or as an annual or in a pot

PLANT Plant seeds, cuttings, or seedlings after the last frost.

SPACE 3 feet (91 cm), or in 2 gallon (7.5 L) pot

CARE Water lightly. Move indoors for the winter. It will drop its leaves but come back in the spring.

HARVEST Harvest leaves after 1 month.

DISEASES/PESTS Pick and spray off pests when necessary.

POINT OF FACT Lemon verbena is native to Argentina and Chile. It is said that lemon verbena has the strongest lemon scent and taste of any lemon-scented herbs.

I GREW IT!

WHEN I GREW IT

DATE

NOTES

Lemongrass

(Cymbopogon citratus)

DESCRIPTION 3–6 foot (91–183 cm) tall grass with long green leaves that have a lemony scent and flavor

HARDY ZONES 9–11, or as an annual or indoor plant

PLANT Plant seedlings after the last frost or anytime in zones 9–11. Lemongrass is also easy to grow from seeds in warm climates.

SPACE 2 feet (61 cm)

CARE Water moderately.

HARVEST Harvest stalks in 3–4 months by breaking off the bottom of a thick stem or picking off leaves.

DISEASES/PESTS Lemongrass will ward away pests but may be affected by blight and other diseases. Avoid overhead watering, and provide good air circulation.

VARIETIES/CULTIVARS Cymbopogon citratus, Cymbopogon flexuosus

POINT OF FACT The tender inner stalk is widely used in Vietnamese and Thai cuisine.

◖ I GREW IT! ▷

WHEN I GREW IT

DATE

NOTES

Mint
(Mentha)

DESCRIPTION 1–2 foot (30.5–61 cm) tall and wide plant with brightly flavored leaves and flowers

HARDY ZONES 4–11

PLANT Plant seedlings or cuttings in a pot.

SPACE 3–4 feet (91–122 cm), or in 2 gallon (7.5 L) pot

CARE Water lightly.

HARVEST Leaves will be ready to harvest roughly a month after planting.

DISEASES/PESTS Spray off bugs with a hose while watering.

VARIETIES/CULTIVARS Applemint, peppermint, spearmint

POINT OF FACT The Romans originally brought mint to England, where it became a staple in the garden. Mint leaves were being used to clean teeth as early as the 6th century.

◗ I GREW IT!

WHEN I GREW IT
DATE

NOTES

....

Mustard
(Brassica juncea)

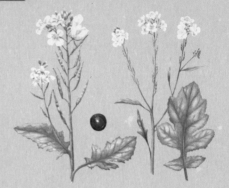

DESCRIPTION 12–18 inch (30.5–45.5 cm) tall and wide plant with leaves grown as greens and seeds used as a spice
NOTE: Allergies to mustard are common.

HARDY ZONES 2–11

PLANT Plant seeds in early spring or late summer. Mustard can tolerate frost.

SPACE 18 inches (45.5 cm)

CARE Water moderately.

HARVEST Harvest leaves after 30–60 days. To harvest seeds, allow the plant to bolt and sprout seeds.

DISEASES/PESTS None.

VARIETIES/CULTIVARS Florida broadleaf, golden frill, red giant

POINT OF FACT Vineyards grow mustard and till it into the soil as mulch for their grape vines. Mustard gets its name from "must"—the old English term for grape juice. Ground seed from the plant was added to the juice so it did not spoil.

I GREW IT!

WHEN I GREW IT
DATE

NOTES

Oregano
(Origanum vulgare)

DESCRIPTION A low-lying, leafy bush with small, flavorful leaves
NOTE: Can cause reactions in people allergic to the Lamiaceae family of plants.

HARDY ZONES 5–10

PLANT Plant seeds or seedlings after the last frost date. Sow a few seeds every 8–12 inches (20.5–30.5 cm).

SPACE 8–12 inches (20.5–30.5 cm)

CARE Water moderately.

HARVEST Harvest leaves anytime.

DISEASES/PESTS Aphids can be controlled by planting catnip nearby or introducing predators such as ladybugs. Spider mites can be sprayed with cold water.

VARIETIES/CULTIVARS Sweet marjoram, pot marjoram

POINT OF FACT The cooler the climate, the less potent oregano will taste.

◦ I GREW IT! ▷

WHEN I GREW IT
DATE

NOTES

....

125

BIENNIAL
Pansy
(Viola tricolor)

DESCRIPTION 6-inch (15 cm) tall plant with edible flowers in white, purple, and yellow

HARDY ZONES 4–11

PLANT Plant seeds or seedlings after the last frost.

SPACE 8–15 inches (20.5–38 cm)

CARE Water moderately. Cut back stems after first bloom to encourage further flowering.

HARVEST Harvest in 85 days.

DISEASES/PESTS Spray pests off plants with a hose.

VARIETIES/CULTIVARS Flirty skirts, monkey face, ultima morpho

POINT OF FACT Shakespeare's *A Midsummer Night's Dream* describes a love potion made from pansy juice. Pansies have both fragrant and scentless varieties.

I GREW IT!

WHEN I GREW IT
DATE

NOTES

Paprika
(Capsicum annuum)

DESCRIPTION 18–36 inch (45.5–91 cm) tall plant that produces chili peppers

HARDY ZONES 9–11, or as an annual in colder climates

PLANT Plant seedlings after the last frost.

SPACE 12 inches (30.5 cm)

CARE Water moderately.

HARVEST Harvest red peppers in about 90 days.

DISEASES/PESTS Peppers are often affected by fungal diseases and root rot. Avoid too much water to prevent these.

VARIETIES/CULTIVARS Hungarian, delicate, special quality

POINT OF FACT Paprika is native to Mexico and South America.

 **I GREW IT!**

WHEN I GREW IT
DATE

NOTES

....

Parsley
(Petroselinum crispum)

to

DESCRIPTION 12–18 inch (30.5–45.5 cm) tall bushy plant with curly edible leaves

HARDY ZONES 4–9

PLANT Plant seeds 3–4 weeks before the last spring frost. Parsley takes a few weeks to sprout.

SPACE 18 inches (45.5 cm)

CARE Water heavily while sprouting, moderately once established.

HARVEST Harvest leaves once they have three segments.

DISEASES/PESTS Parsley is a favorite food of many animals. Insects can be sprayed off, but you may need to share with rabbits and other grazers.

VARIETIES/CULTIVARS Curly leaved, flat leaved, Hamburg

POINT OF FACT The ancient Greeks regarded parsley as a symbol of death. Parsley is high in vitamins A, C, and K.

I GREW IT!

WHEN I GREW IT
DATE

NOTES

PERENNIAL

Rosemary
(Rosmarinus officinalis)

DESCRIPTION 3-foot (91 cm) evergreen herb with sweet, needled branches

HARDY ZONES 7–10; in cooler zones it can be moved indoors for the winter

PLANT Plant seedlings after the last frost.

SPACE 3 feet (91 cm)

CARE Water lightly.

HARVEST Harvest leaves anytime.

DISEASES/PESTS Pests can be sprayed off with water.

VARIETIES/CULTIVARS Marjorca pink, Tuscan blue

POINT OF FACT Rosemary grows in the wild in the Mediterranean region and has been used there as affordable incense. Rosemary's name in Latin means "dew of the sea."

I GREW IT!

WHEN I GREW IT
DATE

NOTES

Sage
(Salvia officinalis)

DESCRIPTION 2-foot (61 cm) tall herb with flavorful leaves

HARDY ZONES 5–8

PLANT Plant sage seedlings after the last frost.

SPACE 2 feet (61 cm)

CARE Water sparsely. The plants become woody after about 4 years, at which point they should be replaced.

HARVEST Harvest leaves a few months after planting.

DISEASES/PESTS Sage is disease-resistant as long as it doesn't become water-logged.

VARIETIES/CULTIVARS golden, purple, tricolor

POINT OF FACT Sage is native to Mexico and the American Southwest. Sage honey is honey made by bees who visit sage flowers.

I GREW IT!

WHEN I GREW IT
DATE

NOTES

PERENNIAL

Shallots

(Allium cepa ascalonicum)

DESCRIPTION 8–16 inch (20.5–40.5 cm) tall plant grown for its mildly onion-flavored bulbs

HARDY ZONES 4–10

PLANT Plant sets in spring or fall with the round (root) end down at a depth of 1 inch (2.5 cm).

SPACE 6 inches (15 cm)

CARE Water heavily after planting, moderately as they mature, and lightly a few weeks before harvest.

HARVEST Harvest in 60–120 days, when the stalks fall over and yellow. Dig up the bulbs, and let them dry for a few weeks before cooking.

DISEASES/PESTS Remove any plants with white rot, which will leave white spots on the stalk.

VARIETIES/CULTIVARS Pikant, matador, bonilla

POINT OF FACT Shallots have a slight garlic-like taste to them and are popular in French cuisine.

I GREW IT!

WHEN I GREW IT
DATE

NOTES

Sichuan (Szechuan) Peppercorn

(Zanthoxylum piperitum)

 to

DESCRIPTION A thorny tree that grows to 13–17 feet (4–5 m) and produces edible peppercorns

HARDY ZONES 6–9

PLANT Plant saplings in spring or fall. A male and female plant are required if fruit is desired.

SPACE 15–20 feet (4.5–6 m)

CARE Water moderately.

HARVEST Harvest fruit after 2 years.

DISEASE/PESTS Sichuan peppercorn trees are pest- and disease-resistant.

POINT OF FACT Szechuan peppercorns are one of the ingredients in five-spice. In Mandarin, the plant is known as *Ma La*, which means "spicy and tingly."

I GREW IT!

WHEN I GREW IT
DATE

NOTES

132

Star Anise
(Illicium verum)

○ to ☾

DESCRIPTION 10-foot (3 m) tall and wide evergreen tree with star-shaped fruit that is dried and ground into spice

HARDY ZONES 7–9, or in a pot that can be moved indoors

PLANT Plant seeds in the fall. First place seeds in water and plant only those that sink.

SPACE 10 feet (3 m)

CARE Water moderately. If growing in a pot, pot up each year. Add fertilizer or compost each year.

HARVEST Harvest fruit after 6 years. Pick unripe fruit in the fall, and let it dry out in the sun until a reddish–brown.

DISEASES/PESTS None; it has antibacterial and pest-repellent properties.

POINT OF FACT The Japanese star anise plant is a close relative but is highly toxic. Star anise is used to make the active ingredient in the medicine Tamiflu.

I GREW IT!

WHEN I GREW IT
DATE

NOTES

PERENNIAL
Tarragon
(Artemisia dracunculus)

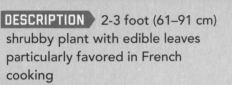

DESCRIPTION 2-3 foot (61–91 cm) shrubby plant with edible leaves particularly favored in French cooking

HARDY ZONES 4–9

PLANT Plant seedlings after the last frost.

SPACE 2 feet (61 cm)

CARE Water moderately. Prune the plant to prevent flowering. Tarragon should be divided and replanted after 4 years.

HARVEST Harvest leaves in the second month after planting. Leaves taste best in the summer.

DISEASES/PESTS Spray off the flies and remove diseased leaves.

VARIETIES/CULTIVARS French

POINT OF FACT Tarragon reached Europe from Siberia in the Middle Ages, where it became a culinary staple.

I GREW IT!

WHEN I GREW IT
DATE

NOTES

Thyme
(Thymus vulgaris)

DESCRIPTION 6–10 inch (15–25 cm) tall herb with flavorful sprigs

HARDY ZONES 5–9

PLANT Plant seedlings after the last frost.

SPACE 6–12 inches (15–30 cm)

CARE Water lightly.

HARVEST Harvest leaves 1–2 months after planting.

DISEASES/PESTS Spray off spider mites and aphids.

VARIETIES/CULTIVARS Lime, lemon frost

POINT OF FACT Thyme flowers will attract bees to your garden. Roman soldiers burned thyme, believing the fumes would make them more courageous in battle.

I GREW IT!

WHEN I GREW IT

DATE

NOTES

Turmeric

(Curcuma longa)

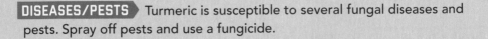

DESCRIPTION 3-foot (91 cm) tall flowering herb whose rhizomes are used in cooking around the world

HARDY ZONES 8–11, or indoors

PLANT Plant 2–3 inch (5–7.5 cm) rhizomes 2 inches (5 cm) deep with a bud facing up.

SPACE 10 inches (25 cm)

CARE Water heavily.

HARVEST Harvest rhizomes 9–10 months after planting. The whole rhizome system can be taken, or some can be left so the plant can survive.

DISEASES/PESTS Turmeric is susceptible to several fungal diseases and pests. Spray off pests and use a fungicide.

VARIETIES/CULTIVARS Alleppey finger, salem, sangli

POINT OF FACT Turmeric has traditionally been used to make golden dye. Turmeric is popular worldwide, but India grows the most varieties.

I GREW IT!

WHEN I GREW IT

DATE

NOTES

Violet
(Viola)

DESCRIPTION Low-lying plant with aromatic and edible purple flowers. They grow wild and as cultivated plants. NOTE: If planted, violets may spread throughout your garden.

HARDY ZONES 3–10

PLANT Plant seedlings or cuttings after the last frost.

SPACE 6–12 inches (15–30.5 cm)

CARE Water heavily. Violets will spread but not take over. They will intersperse themselves among lawn cover. Pull them up by the roots where spreading.

HARVEST Harvest the flowers in spring or summer.

DISEASES/PESTS Violets are mainly affected by spider mites and aphids. Spray these off with a hose or use a natural insecticide.

VARIETIES/CULTIVARS Johnny jump up, majestic giant

POINT OF FACT Violets grow wild and are considered by some to be a weed.

I GREW IT!

WHEN I GREW IT
DATE

NOTES

PART III

VEGETABLES

V. DAWSON

You've seen the posters: "Eat the Rainbow!" "5 Veggies a Day!" Now you are going to do it. And you are going to grow those vegetables yourself! Your mom shows you a sunny patch of grass where you can make a garden. Armed with a shovel, you set out to remove the vegetation and till the soil. Ugh! The ground is hard as a rock! After fifteen minutes of work, you've dug up a single scoop of hard soil. This could take all week! And once finished, how will you plant veggies in these lumps of dirt? *What would you do?*

CHAPTER 1

Leaves, Stems, and Flowers

Vegetables can be classified by the parts of the plant most commonly eaten. They may be grown for their roots, stems, leaves, flowers, or fruit. The first three are self-explanatory. But how can a flower or fruit be a vegetable? Most plants have flowers and fruit, though we may not think of them that way. Not every flower is showy. It is simply the reproductive part of the plant. Broccoli florets and asparagus tips are flowers not yet in bloom, for instance. Likewise, a fruit is simply the part of the plant that produces seeds. When it is sweet (or prepared to be sweet), we also call it a fruit in the informal sense. The vegetable, on the other hand, has no scientific meaning. Rather, it is an informal term for plants that are eaten, whether roots, stems, leaves, flowers, fruit, or some combination.

Among the easiest to grow are plants prized for their leaves, stems, and flowers. These are full of vitamins and often growable year-round. They include lettuce, salad leaves, cabbage, and winter greens.

Lettuce

There are four main types of lettuce: iceberg, romaine, butterhead, and loose leaf. They vary in appearance, but the care is essentially the same. Lettuce likes cool but not freezing temperatures, so plant seeds in early spring or late summer for a spring or fall harvest. If loose leaf (also referred to as cut and come again), individual leaves can be harvested throughout the season. You can do this to some extent with romaine and butterhead, too. Iceberg must be harvested whole. Some people prefer to harvest the whole head of every type of lettuce so that you get the tender leaves at the center. In that case, succession planting—planting a few seeds each week—allows you to harvest heads of lettuce as you are ready for them, instead of all at once. Most lettuce should be planted twelve inches (thirty centimeters) apart. Lettuce can be picked when still "baby lettuce" or allowed to grow to full size. However, once it bolts—grows into a flower—it is too bitter to eat.

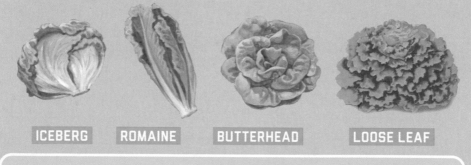

ICEBERG   ROMAINE   BUTTERHEAD   LOOSE LEAF

What Should You Plant?

SWEET TOOTH ▸ These veggies can be baked in breads or pie.
pumpkin, zucchini, rhubarb

HEALTH NUT ▸ These easy-to-grow green veggies can be cooked, mixed in salads, or added to a smoothie.
kale, spinach, Swiss chard

SMALL-SPACE GARDENER ▸ These veggies require 6 inches (15 cm) or less per plant.
carrots, radishes, salad greens

Succession Planting

When you harvest whole heads of lettuce, you can be stuck with too much lettuce. Instead, try succession planting.

WHAT YOU'LL NEED
➢ prepared garden soil and a trowel or spoon

WEEK 1 Prepare a 6-foot (2 m) row for your lettuce. Measure the first 24 inches (61 cm). Plant a pinch of lettuce seeds every 3 inches (7.5 cm). Cover with 0.25 inch (6.5 mm) of soil. Water regularly every week.

WEEK 2 Plant the next 2 feet (61 cm) of the row, as directed above.

WEEK 3 The lettuce in the first section should have sprouted. Plant the final 2 feet (61 cm), as directed above.

WEEK 4 Thin the first part of the row to just a few plants (eventually you will leave just 1 head per foot (30.5 cm).

WEEK 5 Thin the second part of the row, as above.

WEEK 6 AND 7 Thin the third part of the row, as above.

WEEK 8 (FOR LOOSE LEAF) OR WEEK 11 (FOR HEADS) Harvest the first section of lettuce and replant this section, as directed above.

WEEK 9 (LOOSE LEAF) OR WEEK 12 (HEADS) Harvest the second section and replant.

WEEK 10 (LOOSE LEAF) OR WEEK 13 (HEADS) Harvest the third section and replant.

I DID IT! DATE:

Salad Leaves

Often packaged as a "spring mix," other salad leaves include arugula, watercress and land cress, lamb's lettuce (corn salad), spinach or the easier-to-grow perpetual spinach, endives, chicory, and radicchio. The latter three are bitter and so usually mixed with other leaves. Like lettuce, salad leaves prefer cool temperatures, but they are also frost-tolerant. They can be planted in early spring, or late summer for a fall and winter harvest.

ARUGULA

WATERCRESS

LAND CRESS

LAMB'S LETTUCE (CORN SALAD)

SPINACH

PERPETUAL SPINACH

ENDIVES

CHICORY

RADICCHIO

Greens

In terms of cooking, lettuce is prepared cold, and salad leaves, cold or lightly sautéed, whereas greens can withstand heavier cooking—and are delicious that way. In the garden, they prefer cool or even cold temperatures—indeed, greens often taste sweetest after a frost. Popular greens include Swiss chard and mustard as well as cabbage species members kale, kohlrabi, and collards.

SWISS CHARD

MUSTARD

COLLARDS

KOHLRABI

TRACK IT ↘ Winter Greens

If you plant cold-hardy greens, your garden can grow year-round. Note the date of your first frost and list the plants you are still harvesting through the winter!

First frost:

Plants still growing strong:

I DID IT!   DATE:

Cabbages

Cabbage growing in the garden is a picture out of a storybook. It's also a versatile vegetable found in many world cuisines. Its crunchiness raw and silkiness cooked, along with its ability to soak up the flavors around it, make it a popular ingredient in dishes such as kimchi, sauerkraut, coleslaw, bierocks, and colcannon. Cabbage includes many varieties, some of which can tolerate heat and others, cold. If you plant a mixture, cabbage can be grown year-round.

Though the term "cabbage" calls to mind round bundles of silky leaves, the cabbage family includes brussels sprouts, kale, collards, kohlrabi, broccoli, and cauliflower. The yellow flowers they all produce reveal the family resemblance, though the plants are usually harvested before they bloom. Cauliflower and broccoli are grown for their florets, kale and collards for their leaves, and kohlrabi for its leaves and stem base. All share a common pest: root fly. A root fly infestation can be prevented by making a felt collar and fastening it around the bottom of the stem to catch any eggs laid near the plant.

BRUSSELS SPROUTS　　**BROCCOLI**　　**CAULIFLOWER**

TRY IT → Make a Cabbage Collar

WHAT YOU'LL NEED

➢ a piece of cardboard and scissors

STEP 1 Cut cardboard into 12-inch (30 cm) circles with 6-inch.

STEP 2 Cut a line to the center of the circle. Then at the center, cut three very short lines (where the stem will go.)

STEP 3 Fasten the collar around the base of the stem to prevent root fly maggots from burrowing into the root.

I DID IT! DATE:

Cole Crop Diseases and Pests

Cole crops include broccoli, Brussels sprouts, cabbage, cauliflower, collards, kale, kohlrabi, mustard, turnip, and watercress. Because they are closely related, they are affected by the same diseases and pests. Potential diseases include pythium damping off, downy mildew, alternaria leaf spot, black rot and fusarium yellows. In general, planting disease-resistant varieties, proper air circulation and garden spacing, soil drainage, crop rotation, clearing the garden of debris, plus weeding and watering the base of the plants and not the leaves can prevent these diseases. Additionally, raised beds and starting seeds in potting soil can deter damping off. Pests include cabbage maggots, cutworms, flea beetles, and cabbage loopers. Row covers can protect the plants from pests, collars can prevent cutworm, crop rotation can deter cabbage maggots, and cabbage loopers should be hand-picked and destroyed.

Stems

For most plants, stems are simply the appendages on which the more delicious parts grow. But for some, stems are the main event. Rhubarb stems are gently sour and can be sautéed as a side dish or baked (with lots of sugar) in a pie. But don't eat the leaves! They are poisonous. Rhubarb is an easy-to-grow perennial that spreads through rhizomes (underground stems that grow horizontally and put down new roots) and can be divided each year. Celery, on the other hand, is known to be a difficult garden plant. Try growing the easier leaf celery, a variety closer to celery's wild ancestor. It has the same flavor but thinner stems and more leaves.

RHUBARB

CELERY

Floret

Besides cauliflower and broccoli, asparagus and artichokes are famous food florets. Both are perennials (asparagus to zone 3 and artichokes to zone 6). And both are expensive to buy but easy to grow. Asparagus is a beautiful plant, with soft, lush leaves. In spring, new shoots and florets are harvested for food. In contrast, an artichoke plant looks like a thistle—one of its relatives. Its floret is harvested before it blooms into a purple flower.

ASPARAGUS AND ARTICHOKES

Would you like to garden organically? Use this checklist.

☐ My topsoil or potting mix does not contain synthetic fertilizer or pesticides.

☐ If I'm using in-ground soil, I am adding only organic matter or rock materials such as sand and perlite.

☐ My seeds or plants are "non-GMO."

☐ For fertilizer, I am using plant or animal matter instead of synthetic chemicals.

☐ For pest control, I pick off insects, prune the affected area, or spray with organic products only.

Certified organic farmers are also required to avoid contamination from synthetic fertilizers, pesticides, and GMO crops from other farms. If you are growing an organic garden, ask your family not to use weed killer, pesticides, or synthetic fertilizer near your plants. These can be spread by wind and rainwater runoff.

I DID IT! DATE:

Grow Asparagus Year by Year

YEAR 1 Choose a permanent location for asparagus—it can live for 20 years! Dig a trench 12 inches (30.5 cm) wide and 6 inches (15 cm) deep. Add 2 inches of loose soil at the bottom of the trench. Plant crowns 24 inches (61 cm) apart. Fill the trench, being careful not to knock over the asparagus. Allow to grow without harvesting.

YEAR 2 In early spring, remove the dead, woody plant matter. Apply *side dressing*—fertilizer added to the side of the plant after it is already established—to each plant. Allow the asparagus to grow without harvesting.

YEAR 3 In spring, again remove the dead, woody plant matter and apply side dressing. Harvest the new asparagus shoots when they are 6–8 inches (15–20.5 cm) tall and pencil-thick. Don't wait too long! The shoots become too tough to eat if allowed to grow bigger. You can now harvest fresh shoots every spring.

I DID IT! DATE:

CHAPTER 2

Roots and Other Underground Veggies

Underground vegetables tend to be cold, hardy, and easily stored. When few fresh vegetables are available, potatoes, carrots, and onions provide nourishment through the winter. Of these, only carrots are true roots. Potatoes and onions grow underground but are tubers and bulbs, respectively.

A bulb is an enlarged part of the stem that grows underground, just above the roots, to store nutrients. It contains a bud surrounded by fleshy leaves. Examples include onions, garlic, and chives—all members of the lily family. Often, bulbs multiply underground. A tuber is an enlarged part of a stem or root that grows underground and can sprout multiple new plants. An example is the potato. A carrot is a taproot. A taproot is a large central root that grows directly beneath the plant's stem.

Onions

Many of the bulbs we eat are classified as herbs, whereas onions are considered vegetables, perhaps because they are eaten in larger quantities. Growing onions is like growing any of the herb bulbs. Onion sets—small bulbs—are planted in early spring and harvested when the leaves begin to wither and turn brown—late summer. The onions are then dug up and allowed to dry on the ground, or else the leaves are tied together and hung to dry. Once dried, the dirt is brushed off and the onions are ready to store or eat. Many onion varieties produce just one bulb, but the so-called walking onion produces new bulbs where the flower would usually be. These can be eaten or left to replant themselves when the top bulbs droop down to the soil.

Potatoes

Potatoes are a staple food in so many countries that it's hard to believe they originated in a small corner of the world. Native to the Andes Mountains, they were introduced to Europe in the 1500s. Because the potato was different from anything Europeans had seen, it was slow to be accepted. Then small-scale farmers began planting potatoes in fallow fields—land typically left to rest and regain nutrients. They produced plentiful tubers—staving off hunger in times of famine. Eventually, potatoes became the primary food source for many European countries, with a portion of the population—40 percent in Ireland—eating a diet almost entirely of potatoes. Sadly, potato blight in the mid-1800s attacked the crop that Ireland had come to rely on, leading to one of the deadliest famines in history. Today, blight is still an issue for potatoes. However, as a top five food crop in tons produced, the potato continues to feed the world.

You can grow potatoes at home, either in the ground or in a pot. Potatoes can be planted from early to late spring. "First early" potatoes are fast-growing varieties that take up less space than later potatoes, making them the most popular among gardeners. Potatoes are grown from seed potatoes, which are just potatoes that have sprouted "eyes." The eyes grow into flowering plants with an underground root and stem system in which several potatoes grow. That means that from one seed potato, many grow.

Plant Potatoes in a Pot

NOTE: Keep the root and stem system covered with soil, because sun damages potatoes. The process of adding soil around potato plants as they grow is known as earthing up.

> **WHAT YOU'LL NEED**
>
> ➤ a large pot, at least 5 gallons (19 L); potting mix; 2–4 "first early" seed potatoes, such as Irish cobbler, Norland, Mountain rose; an empty egg carton; and a trowel or spoon

STEP 1 Plan to plant your potatoes in early spring.

STEP 2 One month before planting the seed potatoes, place them in an empty egg carton to sprout.

STEP 3 If the potatoes are smaller than an egg, they can be planted whole. Larger potatoes can be cut into pieces so that each has two eyes. Do this 2 days before planting.

STEP 4 On the day of planting, fill the garden pot with 6 inches (15 cm) of potting mix. Plant 4 sprouted potatoes, buds up, and cover with 4 more inches (10 cm) of potting mix.

STEP 5 When the potato plants emerge above the soil, earth up the potatoes. (This means to cover all the plant except the leaves with potting mix or soil.)

STEP 6 Water daily.

STEP 7 At the end of summer, when the potato flowers bloom, the potatoes are ready to harvest. Wait for a dry day. Empty the pot onto the ground and harvest the potatoes.

STEP 8 Allow the potatoes to dry on the ground for 2 hours.

I DID IT! DATE:

Sweet Potatoes

Contrary to what the name and shape suggest, sweet potatoes are not closely related to potatoes. Potatoes are members of the nightshade family, whereas sweet potatoes are in the morning glory family. As such, they are grown differently than potatoes. Instead of seed potatoes, sweet potatoes are grown from slips. These are sprouts that have grown on the sweet potato and then allowed to grow their own roots.

The young plants love the heat, so plant them two weeks after the last frost. If you live in a cooler climate, cover the soil with a black trash bag or tarp to heat it up. Harvest the sweet potatoes with a shovel two weeks before the first frost. Brush off the dirt and cure them in a warm and humid place out of direct sunlight for fourteen days or more, during which time they will sweeten. The easiest way is to poke holes in a plastic grocery bag, add a single layer of sweet potatoes, and then tie the bag and place it in a sunny window. Then transfer the sweet potatoes to storage. To store them, wrap each in a newspaper and place in a cool (but not cold), dry place. Sweet potatoes are best about six weeks after harvesting (which includes both curing and storage time).

Carrots and Other Root Vegetables

Root vegetables are grown from seed and harvested several weeks later with a shovel. They can then be stored in a cool, dry place for several weeks. Carrots are the most well-known root vegetables, though their signature color came late in the game. (Early carrots were white, yellow, purple, and red.) If you are short on space or looking to fill out a vertical garden, radish is among the tiniest of plants—each needs just one inch (2.5 cm) to grow. Other root vegetables include beets, rutabagas, and turnips. For all three, the greens are also edible—they can be sautéed like any other greens.

ROOT VEGETABLES

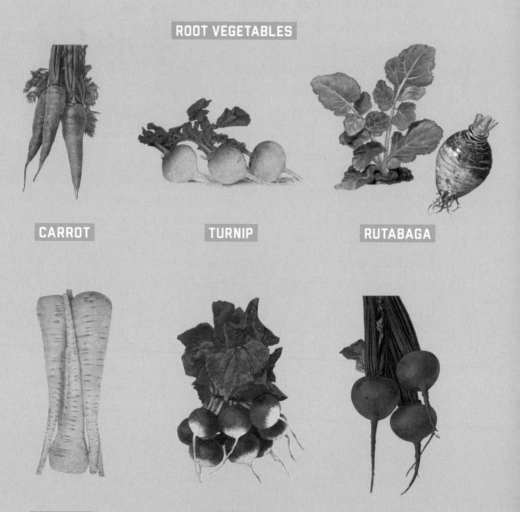

CARROT

TURNIP

RUTABAGA

PARSNIP

RADISH

BEET

CHAPTER 3

Tomatoes and More

Tomatoes are fruits that are vegetables. It may sound confusing, but a fruit is simply the part of the plant that produces seeds. A vegetable is a plant that tastes savory more than sweet. In contrast, an apple is a fruit that is a fruit because it contains seeds AND is sweet.

Yes — Do I have seeds? — No

I am scientifically a fruit.

I am not scientifically a fruit.

Am I sweet or usually prepared to be sweet? — Yes → Then I am a fruit that is a fruit.

No → Then I am a fruit that is commonly called a vegetable.

Tomatoes

Tomatoes are the quintessential garden vegetable. They're easy to grow. They love hot, sunny summers. And they taste much better homegrown than store-bought. Like the potato's, the tomato's wild ancestor is native to South America. Both are members of the nightshade family and, with the greenest of thumbs, can be grafted together to produce a plant that produces tomatoes above ground and potatoes below ground. (Grafting is inserting the upper part of a plant into the root system of another, so that both continue to grow.) Tomatoes range from sugary-sweet cherry tomatoes to giant savory tomatoes and everything in between. All require the same basic care.

WHAT YOU'LL NEED

➤ 9 square feet (8 square m) of garden space with nutrient-rich soil or a 5-gallon (19 L) or larger pot filled with potting mix, liquid fertilizer, a tomato seedling, and a trowel or spoon

STEP 1 Plant the tomato seedling in the garden or pot so that the soil attached to the roots is buried.

STEP 2 Surround the plant with a tomato cage, which will keep it upright as it grows. Alternately, you can drive a stake into the ground next to the tomato and connect the plant to the stake with strips of scrap cloth or twist ties as it grows.

STEP 3 Water the plant moderately (see page 16) right after planting.

STEP 4 Continue to water the plant moderately, soaking the soil when you water and allowing it to dry out in between. For in-ground plants, this will mean watering every 2–7 days, depending on the temperature. Potted plants will need water every 1–2 days.

STEP 5 Once a week, add liquid fertilizer, such as fish emulsion, to the water as directed on the container.

STEP 6 When tomatoes begin to form, the plant will need frequent watering. Watch for wilting, and adjust your watering schedule if needed. Also be mindful of critters. To keep chipmunks, squirrels, and mice away, sprinkle red pepper flakes all around the plant. If they do steal a tomato, leave it on the ground. They may return to that one and leave the ones on the bush alone.

STEP 7 For best results, side dress the tomatoes in 1 month and again 2 months after planting. (Please see sidebar.)

STEP 8 Harvest tomatoes when they are red or whatever color they are supposed to be.

STEP 9 Before the first frost, harvest all green tomatoes. They can be fried or baked into a sweet bread.

I DID IT! DATE:

Side Dressing

Fertilizer is added to the garden before planting. But some plants, particularly fruiting vegetables such as peppers, eggplant, tomatoes, and cucumbers, benefit from fertilizer added throughout the season. Side dressing means sprinkling or pouring fertilizer beside the plant so that it seeps into the soil and is soaked up by the roots. Granular or liquid fertilizer can be used for side dressing. Follow instructions—too much fertilizer damages roots.

Smaller Plants

Plants such as eggplant, peppers, and okra require similar care to tomatoes and can be grown alongside them (provided you give them all enough space).

With its hardy texture and rich flavor, eggplant stars in many dishes. The plant itself is small but prolific. It requires just 4 square feet (4 square m), but during peak harvest (from late summer to the first frost), it bears enough eggplants for a weekly dinner of eggplant parmesan or your favorite eggplant dish.

Peppers may be the only vegetable measured by hotness. Carolina reaper peppers are the hottest variety, whereas sweet peppers are not hot at all. Jalapeños fall somewhere in the middle. Environment also affects peppers' spiciness. The hotter the weather, the hotter the peppers. If you grow peppers, you'll see firsthand that all colors of sweet peppers—and many other varieties—come from the same plant. A green pepper is simply a pepper that hasn't turned red or yellow.

JALAPEÑO PEPPER

HOT HOT HOT!

The hotness of different peppers is measured in Scoville Heat Units. Pure capsaicin, the chemical that makes peppers hot, has the highest rating on the scale.

Pure capsaicin 15,000,000–16,000,000

Police-grade pepper spray 2,500,000–5,300,000

Carolina reaper 2,000,000–2,200,000

Ghost pepper 855,000–1,463,000

Cayenne pepper 30,000–50,000

Jalepeño pepper 2,500–8,000

Peperoncino 100–1,000

Sweet pepper 0–100

CHILLI PEPPER

Veg-tree-bles

Most fruit that grows on trees is sweet. Avocado and olives, on the other hand, are grown for their savory flavors. Avocado can be grown in zones 9–11, or in a greenhouse. It's best to plant a young tree, which will produce fruit in about five years, as opposed to a seed, which may never sprout at all. Olive trees can be grown indoors and moved outside in the summer, at which point the olives will grow.

AVOCADO

TRACK IT ↘ How Hot?

For the scale above, a panel of taste testers sample a mixture of extract from the hot pepper and water and sugar. The score is determined by the amount of water and sugar added so that the taste testers can taste only a hint of heat. Try a modified test.

STEP 1 List each pepper plant you grew.

STEP 2 Chop 1 tablespoon (14.5 mL) and mix it into 1 cup (236.5 mL) of your favorite salsa. Scoop the salsa onto a chip and eat.

STEP 3 Circle one pepper if you can eat one chip with salsa comfortably and then another right away, two if you can eat it but need a break between each chip with salsa, and three if upon eating a chip with salsa, you immediately need to remedy the heat with milk, bread, or another heat stopper.

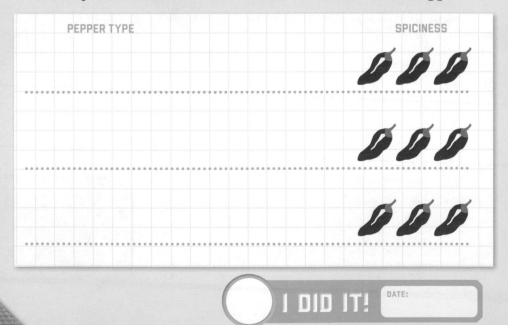

PEPPER TYPE — SPICINESS

I DID IT! DATE:

TRY IT →

Grow an Olive Tree in a Container

WHAT YOU'LL NEED

➢ young, dwarf-variety, self-pollinating olive tree; houseplant fertilizer; an earthenware pot with drainage holes (it should be one size larger than the one it is growing in now); trowel or spoon; and potting mix

STEP 1 Add potting mix to the bottom of the new pot.

STEP 2 Tip the tree out of its current container and place it in the new pot.

STEP 3 Fill in any gaps with more potting soil. Water thoroughly.

STEP 4 Place in a window that gets 6 hours or more of direct sunlight.

STEP 5 Water the tree whenever the soil is dry, 1 inch (2.5 cm) below the surface.

STEP 6 Two weeks after the last frost, set the tree outside in the shade, giving it a little sunlight each day. Increase the amount of sunlight each day.

STEP 7 Once the tree is acclimated, it will enjoy full sun.

STEP 8 Two weeks before the first frost, reverse the acclimation process, moving the tree to the shade a little more each day. When the first frost is expected, move it inside for the winter.

I DID IT! DATE:

CHAPTER 4

Gourds and Melons

Gourds are a family of large fruit that usually grow on vines. Some gourds, like melons, are considered fruit, and some, like cucumbers and squash, are considered vegetables. Decorative but inedible gourds are often referred to as gourds, whereas edible gourds are more commonly called melons, squash, or whatever their name is. Squash are further divided into summer and winter squash. Both grow in summer. The difference is in how long they can be stored. Summer squash can last off the vine for up to two weeks, whereas winter squash will last for several weeks.

Summer Squash

Summer squashes include yellow squash, zucchini, and patty pan squash. All these grow on vines instead of bushy plants, each requiring 9 square feet (8 square m) of space. They can be grown in a container or on a small hill made from garden soil. If they remain free of pests and disease, the plants will produce many squashes for

CROOKNECK AND SCALLOPED SQUASH (OR SUMMER SQUASH)

you to eat. However, vines are vulnerable to boring insects and fungi. Fungus attacks in hot, wet conditions, which often can't be avoided in summer. However, you can help your plant by making sure it gets plenty of sun and not overwatering. Both fungus and insects can be treated with organic spray.

Winter Squash

SQUASH VARIETIES

Acorn, butternut, spaghetti, and pumpkin are all winter squash. They, too, should be grown on hills but require more space, or else scaffolding, for their sprawling vines. Spaghetti squash is unique in that its flesh grows in spaghettilike strands that can be eaten, like pasta, with sauce. The other squashes are similar in texture and flavor, with flesh that is soft and subtly sweet when cooked. They can be roasted, cooked in soups, or baked in pie. The pumpkin holds the record for largest fruit—with extreme specimens weighing more than 1,000 pounds (453.5 kg). But the larger the pumpkin, the poorer the flavor. For cooking, choose smaller varieties.

How Much Room Do You Need to Grow Pumpkins?

Pumpkins should be grown on small mounds formed with garden soil called hills (50 to 100 square feet per hill). They come in vining, semi-bush, and bush varieties, each requiring the following amount of space:

VINING PUMPKINS Allow 5 to 6 feet between hills with 10 to 15 feet between rows

NOTE: You can take advantage of vertical space by growing pumpkins at the top or bottom of a wall or trellis.

SEMI-BUSH PUMPKINS Allow 4 feet between hills with 8 feet between rows

BUSH PUMPKINS Thin to a single plant every 3 feet with 4 to 6 feet between rows

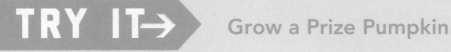

WHAT YOU'LL NEED

➢ garden soil; mulch or manure; a packet of giant variety pumpkin seeds, such as polar bear, big moose, or Dill's Atlantic giant; garden fork or shovel; trowel or spoon; and snips or scissors

STEP 1 Mix the garden soil and mulch or manure.

STEP 2 Plant pumpkins 2 weeks after the last frost or later. If you'd like to time them to be ready in October, plant them in early June.

STEP 3 Choose a sunny spot. With garden soil, make one or more hills 1 foot (30.5 cm) deep and 3 feet (91 cm) across. Follow the space allotments for vining pumpkins (see previous page).

STEP 4 Plant 6 seeds per hill.

STEP 5 Water moderately.

STEP 6 When the seeds sprout, thin to 2 plants per hill.

STEP 7 Once the plants are about 1 foot (30.5 cm) long, thin to 1 plant per hill.

STEP 8 Water deeply twice a week.

STEP 9 Watch for female flowers to appear. They grow after the male flowers, and each has a tiny pumpkin growing at their base. Allow about 3 female flowers to grow. Pinch the others off (and prepare and eat them, see page 168).

STEP 10 When the pumpkins are softball size, choose the healthiest. Pinch off the other 2 pumpkins. Now all the nutrients in the plant will go to that 1 pumpkin. Watch it grow!

STEP 11 Harvest your pumpkin when it is fully mature, that is, when the stem dries out and the pumpkin reaches its final color (usually orange!). Leave the stem attached for better keeping.

◯ **I DID IT!** DATE:

TRACK IT ↘ Prize Pumpkin's Progress

Measure and record your pumpkin's diameter week by week. Wrap a soft tape measure or string around the pumpkin's widest part. If using a string, measure the section of string with a ruler. Be sure to include your unit of measurement (inches or centimeters).

WEEK 1

WEEK 2

WEEK 3

WEEK 4

WEEK 5

WEEK 6

WEEK 7

WEEK 8

| WEEK 9 |
| WEEK 10 |
| WEEK 11 |
| WEEK 12 |
| WEEK 13 |
| WEEK 14 |
| WEEK 15 |
| WEEK 16 |

I DID IT! DATE:

TAKE IT TO THE **NEXT LEVEL** ↗

Harvest and Eat Squash Blossoms

WHAT YOU'LL NEED

➢ squash growing in the garden, scissors or snips, pan, and butter or olive oil

Squash and pumpkin blossoms are edible and delicious. Both male and female flowers grow on squash plants. Pollen from the male flower is spread to female flowers, which then become squash. Leave 2 male flowers on the plant for this purpose. Snip off the others at their base. If you are growing a giant pumpkin, you can also snip off most of the female flowers on that plant. Otherwise, you'll want to leave them growing so that you get more squash. Panfry the squash blossoms in butter or olive oil for a delicious treat.

I DID IT! DATE:

Melons

Melons are also members of the squash family. They, too, grow on ground-hugging vines that require lots of space or heavy-duty scaffolding. In fact, you will grow them in much the same way as pumpkins, which is why we mention them here, though they are considered by everyone to be fruit. Think of them as the sweeter, juicier counterpart to squash. Varieties include watermelon, honeydew, and cantaloupe, all grown basically the same way.

Cucumbers

Cucumbers are grown in much the same way as vining squash. However, they don't need quite as much space. If you provide them with a trellis on which to grow, they can be planted 18 inches (45.5 cm) apart. Cucumbers are prolific. One or two plants will provide you with more than enough cucumbers. Watch your cucumbers carefully. They grow fast, and when larger than their designated size, taste bad.

TAKE IT TO THE NEXT LEVEL ↗

Make Refrigerator Pickles

Fruit and vegetables can be preserved through the process of canning—preparing food so that it can be stored safely in airtight jars. For shorter-term storage, "refrigerator" recipes involve brining or cooking the vegetable but not the second step of boiling the jars. Refrigerator pickles, jams, and apple butter stay fresh for 2 weeks and are a good first step in learning how to can.

➤ 4 clean quart jars, knife and cutting board, measuring spoons and cups, and 1 pound (0.5 kg) of cucumbers, carrots, or other crisp, raw-eaten vegetables

Spices and herbs:

    4 cloves garlic

    4 tsp (8.5 g) dill seed

    4 tsp (7 g) red pepper flakes

    4 tsp (8 g) mustard seed

    4 tsp (11.5 g) peppercorns

Brine:

    1 cup (236.5 mL) vinegar

    1 cup (236.5 mL) water

    0.25 cup (50 g) sugar

    1 T (18 g) salt

STEP 1 Slice vegetables widthwise or lengthwise.

STEP 2 Divide evenly into the 4 jars.

STEP 3 Divide the spices and herbs evenly between the 4 jars.

STEP 4 Boil the brine, and pour evenly into the jars.

STEP 5 Seal the jars, and store in the refrigerator for 2–4 weeks.

I DID IT! DATE:

CHAPTER 5

Pods and Grains

Pods are pouches filled with seeds. Garden favorites include beans, peas, and okra. Green beans grow on bushes (bush beans) or vines (pole beans). As the name suggests, the latter needs a pole or trellis on which to climb. Plant beans two weeks after the last frost. They will be ready to harvest in two months, and then will provide beans until the fall. Okra, a heat-loving plant, should also be planted after the last frost. Peas can be planted much earlier—four weeks before your last frost. They can also be grown in the fall.

Corn, squash, and beans are all native to America. Long ago, Iroquois farmers learned that the three crops grew together in harmony. The corn supplies scaffolding on which the beans can grow. The squash provides ground cover to deter weeds. Note that this method was used on large farms, and as such, requires quite a bit of space.

Three sisters garden

TRY IT → Make a Pole Bean Fort

WHAT YOU'LL NEED

➤ four 8-foot long (2.5 m) poles with a diameter of 0.5-inch (12.5 mm) or narrower (bamboo works well); 1 package pole bean seeds; large garden plot or garden soil; trowel or spoon; stepladder; and string or cord

STEP 1 In a sunny location, measure a 4-foot (122 cm) square. This can be in the garden, if you have room, or in your yard.

STEP 2 At each point, drive a pole into the ground about 6 inches (15 cm) deep, so that the poles tilt slightly toward the middle.

STEP 3 Standing on the stepladder, gather the tops of the poles at the center and tie them together 6 inches (15 cm) from the end.

STEP 4 If the fort will be in the grass, add garden soil 8 inches (20.5 cm) deep around each pole.

STEP 5 For each pole, plant 6 pole bean seeds, 1 inch (2.5 cm) deep.

STEP 6 Water moderately to heavily.

STEP 7 In about a week the seeds will sprout. Thin to 3 plants per pole.

STEP 8 As they grow, gently guide the plants up the poles until they begin to grow up the poles on their own.

STEP 9 Pick pods when beans swell.

I DID IT! DATE:

TAKE IT TO THE NEXT LEVEL ↗

Plant a Three Sisters Garden

WHAT YOU'LL NEED

➢ a garden plot 16x16 feet (5x5 m), garden soil, and a packet each of corn, squash, and pole bean seeds

STEP 1 Measure 16 4x4 foot (122x122 cm) squares. In a checkerboard pattern, create an approximately 4x4x1 foot (122x122x30.5 cm) mound of garden soil in every other square. You will plant corn and beans in 2 rows and squash in 2 rows.

STEP 2 For the corn and bean rows. Plant 10 corn kernels 1 foot (30.5 cm) apart. When the corn grows to 5 inches (12.5 cm), plant 3 beans next to each cornstalk.

STEP 3 In the squash rows, plant a few squash seeds. Thin to 2 plants per mound. Allow the vine to sprawl out over the garden.

STEP 4 Water all moderately to heavily.

I DID IT! DATE:

TRY IT → Mulch Your Garden

Adding mulch around large plants or between rows of small plants suppresses weeds and traps moisture. You can use mulch from the garden store, grass clippings, or straw.

> **WHAT YOU'LL NEED**
>
> ➤ wood chips, grass clippings, or straw (see below for the amount); a wheelbarrow; a shovel or pitchfork; a garden rake; and a helper

STEP 1 Calculate how much mulch you need. Mulch is sold in cubic yards. Use this formula: [(area in square feet) x (3 inches of mulch)] ÷ 324 = (the number of cubic yards needed).

STEP 2 Fill a wheelbarrow with the mulch. Have your helper push the wheelbarrow forward while you use a shovel or pitchfork to scoop the mulch onto the space between your garden rows.

STEP 3 Use the garden rake to spread the mulch 3 inches (7.5 cm) thick in between the garden rows and around large plants.

NOTE: If mulch is not in your budget, you can simply weed between the rows or lay down cardboard.

I DID IT!   DATE:

Grains

Grains are less common in the garden because of the scale needed to produce usable amounts. Corn is an exception as it is also eaten as a fresh vegetable. Though it takes up a lot of space, corn is rewarding to grow. For one thing, it's sweetest when eaten fresh. (As soon as it is picked, the sugars turn to starch.) Second, it grows tall and fast—some farmers say you can hear it growing. Third, it's the quintessential American plant, with at least 6,000 years of domestication on the continent. It may be tempting to plant corn in the back row of the garden, but it's best to plant it in blocks of at least three rows to allow for pollination.

Unique Veggies to Grow

ACHOCHA A relative of cucumber, this easy-to-grow plant tastes like green peppers but can be grown in cooler climates.

CUCAMELON This vining plant produces tiny fruit that look like watermelon but taste like cucumber.

HOSTA A go-to perennial for shady spots, hostas are also edible. Their asparagus-tasting leaves and stems are best when young and tender.

JICAMA They look like potatoes but are eaten raw. NOTE: Only the root is edible—the rest of the plant is poisonous.

RAT-TAILED RADISH All radishes produce edible pods if left in the ground long enough, but rat-tailed radish has been bred specifically for tasty and dramatic-looking pods.

STRAWBERRY SPINACH Aptly named, this plant has leaves that can be eaten like spinach, and berries, like strawberries!

VEGETABLE GUIDE

Rows of lettuce, carrots, and tomatoes make a picture-perfect garden! They are also rewarding to grow, because most are ready to harvest within a few months. Choose a few of your favorites, and dig in!

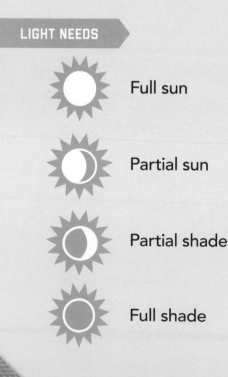

Full sun

Partial sun

Partial shade

Full shade

Achocha

(Cyclanthera pedate or *Cyclanthera brachystachya)*

DESCRIPTION A 6-foot (1.8 m) vine with edible pepper-shaped fruit

HARDY ZONES 7–13

PLANT Plant 2 seeds per small pot in late spring. After the last frost, transplant the seedlings in garden beds, lightly affixing them to a trellis or other support.

SPACE 3 feet (91 cm)

CARE Water moderately. While fruits develop, apply a high-potassium fertilizer.

HARVEST Harvest fruit in 90–110 days.

DISEASES/PESTS Achocha is pest- and disease-resistant.

VARIETIES/CULTIVARS *brachystachya* is known as fat baby, *pedata* is known as lady's slipper

POINT OF FACT Achocha is also known as Caigua, Caihua, Caygua, Korila, and Wild Cucumber.

I GREW IT!

WHEN I GREW IT

DATE

NOTES

Arugula
(Eruca vesicaria)

DESCRIPTION 1–2 feet (30.5–61 cm) tall plant with peppery leaves used in salads

HARDY ZONES 2–11

PLANT Plant seeds after the last frost date.

SPACE 6 inches (15 cm)

CARE Water heavily. Arugula tolerates light overnight freezes as long as daytime temperatures are above 40°F (4°C).

HARVEST Harvest young, tender leaves in 21–40 days. Flower buds and petals are edible as well.

DISEASES/PESTS Arugula is pest- and disease-resistant.

VARIETIES/CULTIVARS Apollo, astro II, sylvetta

POINT OF FACT Arugula is also called rocket or roquette. It was first grown by the ancient Greeks and Romans. In ancient Greece, arugula was used as a medicine.

I GREW IT!

WHEN I GREW IT
DATE

NOTES

....

179

Asparagus

(Asparagus officinalis)

DESCRIPTION 3–4 foot (91–122 cm) tall and wide fern with edible shoots

HARDY ZONES 3–10

PLANT Plant crowns (young plants) in early spring.

SPACE 18 inches (46 cm)

CARE Water moderately.

HARVEST Harvest crowns in the second or third year, when they are 6–8 inches (15–20.5 cm) tall and 0.5 inch (12.5 mm) thick, by cutting at the soil line.

DISEASES/PESTS Asparagus is pest- and disease-resistant.

VARIETIES/CULTIVARS Jersey giant, Mary Washington, Jersey king

POINT OF FACT White and green asparagus come from the same plant. Lack of sunlight inhibits photosynthesis in white asparagus, so the stalks never turn green. Humans have been cultivating asparagus for more than 2,500 years.

I GREW IT!

WHEN I GREW IT
DATE

NOTES

BIENNIAL GROWN AS AN ANNUAL

Beet
(Beta vulgaris)

to

DESCRIPTION 2–3 foot (61–91 cm) tall plant with edible red roots

HARDY ZONES 3–10

PLANT Plant seeds 30 days before the last spring frost in zones 3–7. In zones 8–10, sow seeds in the summer.

SPACE 3–4 inches (7.5–10 cm)

CARE Water moderately.

HARVEST Harvest 7–8 weeks after planting. Dig beetroots out of the soil when they reach the desired size.

DISEASES/PESTS Protect your beets from beet-leaf miners and other pests with row covers.

VARIETIES/CULTIVARS Red ace, Detroit dark red, formanova

POINT OF FACT Among vegetables, beets have the highest sugar content. Beets are the main ingredient in borscht, a common Eastern European soup.

WHEN I GREW IT
DATE

NOTES

....

Broccoli

(Brassica oleracea var. italica)

DESCRIPTION 1.5–2 foot (45.5–61 cm) tall green plant with an edible flowering head

HARDY ZONES 2–11

PLANT Plant seeds 2–3 weeks before the last spring frost date, or 85–100 days before the first fall frost.

SPACE 12 inches (30.5 cm)

CARE Water heavily. Use fertilizer 3 weeks after planting.

HARVEST Harvest 60–90 days after planting. Cut the florets, along with at least 6 inches (15 cm) of the stem.

DISEASES/PESTS See cole crop diseases and pests (page 148).

VARIETIES/CULTIVARS green goliath

POINT OF FACT A cup of broccoli has a little less calcium than a cup of milk. It is also high in vitamin A, potassium, folic acid, iron, and fiber.

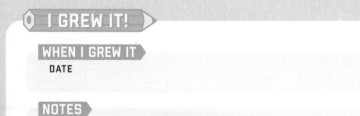

I GREW IT!

WHEN I GREW IT

DATE

NOTES

ANNUAL

Brussels Sprouts
(Brassica oleracea var. gemmifera)

DESCRIPTION 2–3 foot (61–91 cm) tall plant with cabbage-like edible buds

HARDY ZONES 2–11

PLANT Plant seeds about 4 months before the first fall frost date.

SPACE 12–24 inches (30.5–61 cm)

CARE Water heavily. Side dress with fertilizer 3 weeks after transplanting.

HARVEST Harvest sprouts when they reach about 1 inch (2.5 cm) in diameter. They have a better flavor after the first fall frost.

DISEASES/PESTS See cole crop diseases and pests (page 148).

VARIETIES/CULTIVARS Jade cross, Long Island improved, valiant, ruby crunch

POINT OF FACT Brussels sprouts get their name from their popularity in Brussels, Belgium, in the 1300s. In 2013, a group of students and scientists in London used 1,000 Brussels sprouts to power Christmas lights.

I GREW IT!

WHEN I GREW IT
DATE

NOTES

ANNUAL OR BIENNIAL

Cabbage

(Brassica oleracea var. capitate)

DESCRIPTION 1–2 foot (30.5–61 cm) tall vegetable grown for its edible leaves

HARDY ZONES 2–11

PLANT Plant seedlings after the last frost, or plant seeds in late summer for a fall harvest.

SPACE 12–24 inches (30.5–61 cm)

CARE Water heavily. Fertilize the soil 3 weeks after transplanting. Use mulch to protect the shallow roots of the plants and retain moisture in the soil.

HARVEST Harvest 70 days after planting. Cut the cabbage head at the base.

DISEASES/PESTS Row covers can protect the plants from pests, collars can prevent cutworm, crop rotation can deter cabbage maggots, and cabbage loopers should be handpicked and destroyed.

VARIETIES/CULTIVARS Ruby perfection, blue vantage, stonehead, early jersey wakefield

POINT OF FACT According to *Guinness World Records*, the heaviest cabbage was 127 pounds (57.5 kg).

I GREW IT!

WHEN I GREW IT
DATE

NOTES

Carrot
(Daucus carota var. sativus)

DESCRIPTION 3–36 inch (7.5–91 cm) tall vegetable with feathery leaves and edible taproots

HARDY ZONES 2–11

PLANT Plant seeds outdoors 3–5 weeks before the last frost.

SPACE 3 inches (7.5 cm)

CARE Water moderately.

HARVEST Harvest carrots in 2–4 months. Gently lift the carrot from the soil. They are frost-resistant and taste best after a cold snap.

DISEASES/PESTS Carrots are pest- and disease-resistant.

VARIETIES/CULTIVARS Nantes, danvers, little finger

POINT OF FACT Wild carrot is also known as Queen Anne's lace, for its delicate white flowers. Early carrots were red, purple, black, or white.

I GREW IT!

WHEN I GREW IT
DATE

NOTES

BIENNIAL GROWN AS AN ANNUAL

Cauliflower

(Brassica oleracea var. botrytis)

DESCRIPTION 1–2.5 foot (30.5–76 cm) tall cool-weather vegetable with a head of white florets eaten as a vegetable

HARDY ZONES 2–11

PLANT Start seeds 6–8 weeks before the spring frost. Plant 0.5 inch (12.5 mm) deep and 3–6 inches (7.5–15 cm) apart. Transplant the seedlings 4–5 weeks later, 18–24 inches (45.5–61 cm) apart and 30 inches (76 cm) between rows.

SPACE 18–24 inches (45.5–61 cm)

CARE Water heavily. Side dress the plants with nitrogen fertilizer.

HARVEST Cauliflower takes 75–85 days after transplant for heads to form. When the head is 2–3 inches (5–7.5 cm) in diameter, blanch the plant. Blanching is protecting part of a plant from the sun to improve the flavor and appearance. Tie the outer leaves together over the head with twine to blanch the plant. Then, 7–12 days after blanching, harvest the heads by cutting them off with a large knife.

DISEASES/PESTS See cole crop pests and diseases (page 148).

VARIETIES/CULTIVARS Snowball, orange bouquet

POINT OF FACT Cauliflower really is a flower.

I GREW IT!

WHEN I GREW IT
DATE

NOTES

186

Celery

(Apium graveolens var. dulce)

DESCRIPTION 2–2.5 foot (61–76 cm) tall plant with edible stalks eaten as a vegetable

HARDY ZONES 3–6

PLANT Plant seedlings outside after the last frost, or start seeds indoors 8–12 weeks before the average last frost date. Seeds should be soaked in warm water overnight to reduce germination time.

SPACE 12 inches (30.5 cm)

CARE Water heavily. Side dress in the second and third month of growth with a 5-10-10 fertilizer.

HARVEST Celery is ready in 100–130 days. Stalks can be picked once they reach 8 inches (20.5 cm) tall.

DISEASES/PESTS Celery diseases, such as pink rot, black heart, and blight, can be prevented by adding magnesium and calcium to the soil.

VARIETIES/CULTIVARS French dinant, golden self-blanching, Utah 52-70R improved

POINT OF FACT Wild celery appears in Homer's *The Iliad* and *The Odyssey*.

◖ I GREW IT! ▷

WHEN I GREW IT
DATE

NOTES

....

Chickpea
(Cicer arietinum)

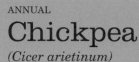

DESCRIPTION 8–40 inch (20.5–101.5 cm) tall plant with 1-inch (2.5 cm) wide pods that contain 1–2 large seeds that are eaten or ground into hummus

HARDY ZONES Any place with mild summers. Temperature should range from 50–85°F (10–29°C) for at least 3 months.

PLANT Plant seeds 1.5–2 inches (4–5 cm) deep, 3–4 inches (7.5–10 cm) apart, 1–2 weeks before the last frost date.

SPACE 10–18 inches (25.5–45.5 cm)

CARE Water moderately.

HARVEST Harvest 100 days after planting. To eat the pods fresh, harvest them while they are small and green. To harvest the seeds, pull the plant down when the leaves turn brown, then lay the plant on a flat, warm surface and allow the pods to dry and split.

DISEASES/PESTS Diseases include Ascochyta blight, Rhizoctonia root rot, pythium rot, fusarium wilt, white mold, bacterial blight, and certain viruses.

VARIETIES/CULTIVARS Kabuli, desi

POINT OF FACT Another name for chickpeas is garbanzo beans.

I GREW IT!

WHEN I GREW IT
DATE

NOTES

Chicory
(Cichorium intybus)

DESCRIPTION 2–4 foot (61–122 cm) tall cool-season plant commonly eaten as a vegetable

HARDY ZONES 3–8

PLANT In warmer climates, sow in September through May. For cooler climates, the seeds should be planted 3–4 weeks after the last spring frost date. Plant seeds as directed on packet.

SPACE 18–24 inches (45.5–61 cm)

CARE Water moderately. Side dress 4 weeks after transplanting.

HARVEST Harvest leaves or full heads 85–100 days after planting to mature.

DISEASES/PESTS Remove slugs and snails by hand or with a potato trap.

VARIETIES/CULTIVARS Rossa di Treviso, Rossa di Verona, firebird

POINT OF FACT Chicory roots can be used as a replacement for coffee beans to make coffee.

I GREW IT!

WHEN I GREW IT
DATE

NOTES

PERENNIAL

Chili Peppers

(Capsicum annuum)

DESCRIPTION 1–2.5 foot (30.5–76 cm) tall shrub with spicy fruit eaten raw, cooked, or ground into a spice

HARDY ZONES 9–11, or in lower zones as an annual or houseplant

PLANT Plant seedlings after last frost, or plant seeds indoors 6–8 weeks before the last frost date and transplant outside.

SPACE 18–36 inches (45.5–91 cm)

CARE Water moderately.

HARVEST Harvest peppers 75 days after planting seeds, or 35 days after planting seedlings. At its peak ripeness, the color is most vivid.

DISEASES/PESTS Aphids can be controlled with a solution of dish soap and water or by introducing ladybugs as a predator.

VARIETIES/CULTIVARS Ancho, cayenne, jalapeño

POINT OF FACT Chili peppers were domesticated in Mexico 6,000 years ago.

 **I GREW IT!**

WHEN I GREW IT
DATE

 NOTES

BIENNIAL GROWN AS AN ANNUAL

Collard Greens

(Brassica oleracea var. acephala)

DESCRIPTION 20–36 inch (51–91 cm) tall plant with rosettes of dark green leaves that are cooked and eaten

HARDY ZONES 2–11

PLANT Sow seeds after the last frost, or in the fall 8–12 weeks before the average first frost date.

SPACE 18 inches (45.5 cm)

CARE Water moderately.

HARVEST Harvest leaves in 55–75 days. Harvest whole plants or bottom leaves as needed. A light frost produces a sweeter flavor.

DISEASES/PESTS See cole family diseases (page 148).

VARIETIES/CULTIVARS Champion, flash, Georgia LS

POINT OF FACT Collards are one of the oldest greens in the cabbage family. They are native to the Mediterranean region.

I GREW IT!

WHEN I GREW IT
   DATE

NOTES

191

Corn
(Zea mays)

DESCRIPTION 4–12 foot (1.2–3.7 m) tall stalk with 1–2 ears of corn growing on the side

HARDY ZONES 2–11

PLANT Plant seeds after the last frost as directed on the seed pack. Corn requires a minimum of 12 plants grown in 1 area to ensure proper pollination.

SPACE 12–18 inches (30.5–45.5 cm)

CARE Water moderately. Side dress the garden with aged compost when the stalks are 10 inches (25.5 cm) tall, when they are 18 inches (45.5 cm) tall, and again when they tassel.

HARVEST Corn is ready to harvest 20 days after the silk first begins growing, or 60–110 days after planting. To harvest, grab the ear, twist, and pull downward.

DISEASES/PESTS Corn pests include cutworms, wireworms, flea beetles, corn earworms, and corn borers. Place one drop of mineral oil in the tip of each ear to kill earworms. (Note: Wait till after pollination to apply.) Corn borers can be controlled with handpicking. Wood ash and agricultural lime can prevent flea beetles.

VARIETIES/CULTIVARS Bodacious, kandy korn, how sweet it is

POINT OF FACT Corn was domesticated in Mexico from the wild grass teosinte about 10,000 years ago.

I GREW IT!

WHEN I GREW IT
DATE

NOTES

ANNUAL

Cucumber

(Cucumis sativus)

DESCRIPTION 9–18 inch (23–45.5 cm) with a 3–8 foot vine (0.9–2.5 m) with fruits commonly eaten as a vegetable

HARDY ZONES 2–11

PLANT Plant seeds after the last frost date.

SPACE 1.5 feet (45.5 cm)

CARE Water moderately until fruit forms, and then heavily.

HARVEST Harvest cucumbers in 55–65 days.

DISEASES/PESTS Pests include aphids, cucumber beetles, and squash bugs. Spray off bugs or pick them off by hand.

VARIETIES/CULTIVARS Burpless bush hybrid, Boston pickling, calypso

POINT OF FACT Cucumbers were first domesticated in India more than 3,000 years ago. The inside of a cucumber can be 20°F (-7°C) cooler than the outside temperature, hence the phrase "cool as a cucumber."

 **I GREW IT!**

WHEN I GREW IT
DATE

NOTES

Eggplant
(Solanum melongena)

 to

DESCRIPTION 2–4 foot (61–122 cm) tall plant that produces edible oval or cylindrical fruit that is eaten as a vegetable

HARDY ZONES 9–12, or as an annual

PLANT Plant seedlings after the last frost, or sow seeds indoors to be transplanted. Plant seedlings 2–2.5 feet (61–76 cm) apart in rows 3–4 feet (91–122 cm) apart.

SPACE 2–2.5 feet (61–76 cm)

CARE Water moderately.

HARVEST Harvest fruit 65–80 days after transplanting. It should be shiny and uniform in color.

DISEASES/PESTS Pick off tomato hornworms or spray with an insecticidal soap.

VARIETIES/CULTIVARS Black beauty, early bird, ichiban

POINT OF FACT While it is eaten as a vegetable, eggplant is actually a berry. Though most modern eggplants are a dark purple, the plant got its name from 18th-century cultivars that had small, white fruit.

 I GREW IT!

WHEN I GREW IT
DATE

NOTES

Endive

(Cichorium endivia)

DESCRIPTION 12-inch (30.5 cm) tall vegetable with crinkled leaves eaten in salads

HARDY ZONES 3–10

PLANT Plant seeds in early spring and again in late summer. Sow seeds 0.25 inch (6.5 mm) deep and 4 inches (10 cm) apart, in rows 12 inches (30.5 cm) apart.

SPACE 8–12 inches (20–30 cm)

CARE Water moderately. The bitterness of endive can be reduced by blanching. When leaves are 10 inches (25.5 cm) tall (40 days), tie the leaves together or cover with a large pot for 3 weeks.

HARVEST Harvest leaves in 10–11 weeks.

DISEASES/PESTS Handpick slugs or set potato traps to catch them.

VARIETIES/CULTIVARS Frisée, escarole

POINT OF FACT Endive is high in folate, vitamins A and K, and fiber.

I GREW IT!

WHEN I GREW IT
DATE

NOTES

Globe Artichoke
(Cynara cardunculus var. scolymus)

DESCRIPTION 3–4 foot (91–122 cm) tall and wide plant with silvery-green leaves and thick stems topped with large, edible pinecone-like flower buds that are eaten as a vegetable
NOTE: Fully open buds are inedible.

HARDY ZONES 6–9

PLANT Plant suckers (or root pieces) in March and April.

SPACE 2–3 feet (61–91 cm)

CARE Water moderately. Divide the plant every 3 years to keep it productive. Cover the plants over the winter.

HARVEST Harvest buds starting in the second year. The artichokes are ready to harvest when they are at least 3 inches (7.5 cm) in diameter.

DISEASES/PESTS Pests include slugs, snails, and aphids. Slugs and snails can be handpicked or controlled with traps. Aphids can be sprayed off.

VARIETIES/CULTIVARS Green globe, imperial star

POINT OF FACT The scientific name for artichoke comes from mythical Cynara, whom Zeus fell in love with but then turned into an artichoke.

I GREW IT!

WHEN I GREW IT
DATE

NOTES

ANNUAL
Green Beans
(Phaseolus vulgaris)

DESCRIPTION 2–10 foot (0.5–3 m) tall bush or vine that grows long, edible pods

HARDY ZONES 2–11

PLANT Plant seeds after the last frost, or in the fall 10–12 weeks before first frost.

SPACE 4–6 inches (10–15 cm)

CARE Water moderately. Pole bean varieties require a trellis or teepee for support. Side dress with compost halfway through the growing season.

HARVEST Harvest beans as soon as they are firm but before the seeds begin the bulge. For bush varieties, this is usually 50–55 days; for poles, 55–65 days.

DISEASES/PESTS Spray insects off. To remove aphids, leafhoppers, and mites, spray the pests off with the hose.

VARIETIES/CULTIVARS Kentucky wonder (pole), bountiful (bush), romano (bush or pole)

POINT OF FACT Green beans are also known as string beans because of the fibrous string that ran the length of the pod in older varieties. Today, most green beans are stringless.

◖ I GREW IT! ▷

WHEN I GREW IT
   DATE

NOTES

....

197

ANNUAL
Fava Beans
(Vicia faba)

 to

DESCRIPTION 2–7 foot (0.5–2 m) tall upright plant with rounded leaves and bean pods that are grown for food

HARDY ZONES 2–10

PLANT In zones 6 and up, fava beans should be sown in fall to grow in winter, while in colder regions the seeds should be sown in the spring. Seeds should be sown 1–2 inches (2.5–5 cm) deep and 7 inches (17.5 cm) apart, in rows 5 inches (12.5 cm) apart.

SPACE 8 inches (20.5 cm)

CARE Water moderately. Fava beans are frost-tolerant, but seedlings should be covered to protect from hard freezes, and plants should be covered for protection from too much frost and snow.

HARVEST Fava beans are ready for harvest in 75–80 days.

DISEASES/PESTS Spray insects with the hose. Diseases include blight, mosaic, and anthracnose. Plant disease-resistant varieties; destroy infected plants.

VARIETIES/CULTIVARS Aquadulce claudia, windsor, The Sutton

POINT OF FACT In New Orleans, fava beans are blessed and given out on St. Joseph's Day (March 19) to celebrate the saint bringing rainfall during drought.

I GREW IT!

WHEN I GREW IT
DATE

NOTES

Jerusalem Artichoke

(Helianthus tuberosus)

DESCRIPTION 5-foot (1.5 m) tall species of sunflower with small yellow flowers and edible tubers that can be cooked like a potato or eaten raw like water chestnuts NOTE: Only the tubers are edible.

HARDY ZONES 2–9

PLANT Plant small, budded tuber pieces in early spring, as soon as the ground can be worked. Plant at a depth of 2–3 inches (5–7.5 cm) and 12–18 inches (30.5–45.5 cm) apart.

SPACE 2 feet (61 cm)

CARE Water moderately.

HARVEST Dig up tubers when the flowers begin to die, 105–140 days after planting. The tubers can be harvested all winter.

DISEASES/PESTS Jerusalem artichokes are disease- and pest-resistant. The main issue is keeping them under control, as a new plant can grow from the smallest piece of tuber left in the soil after harvest.

VARIETIES/CULTIVARS French mammoth white, sugarball, fuseau

POINT OF FACT The tubers contain inulin rather than the carbohydrates found in potatoes. During digestion, inulin breaks down into fructose, not glucose.

I GREW IT!

WHEN I GREW IT
DATE

NOTES

Jicama
(Pachyrhizus erosus)

DESCRIPTION A climbing plant up to 16 feet (5 m) long with blue or white flowers, pods, and edible tubers NOTE: Only the tubers are edible. All parts of the plant grown above the ground are toxic.

HARDY ZONES 7–10

PLANT Plant seeds indoors 6–8 weeks before the last spring frost date. First, soak seeds in water for 12 hours, then sow in a 3-inch (7.5 cm) pot at a depth of 2 inches (5 cm). After the danger of frost has passed, plant outdoors 8 inches (20.5 cm) apart and in rows 24 inches (61 cm) apart. Harden the plants by covering them at night for the first 2 weeks.

SPACE 8 inches (20.5 cm)

CARE Water moderately. Once blooms begin to appear, apply a liquid tomato fertilizer once a week.

HARVEST Dig up the tubers after about 150 days and before the first frost.

DISEASES/PESTS Jicama plants are generally disease- and pest-free.

VARIETIES/CULTIVARS agua dulce, cristalina, San Juan

POINT OF FACT The word *jicama* comes from the Náhuatl word *xīcama*.

◊ I GREW IT!

WHEN I GREW IT
DATE

NOTES

Kale

(Brassica oleracea var. sabellica)

DESCRIPTION 2-foot (61 cm) tall plant with ruffled leaves used in salads or cooking

HARDY ZONES 2–11

PLANT Plant from early spring to early summer and again in the fall, 6–8 weeks before the first expected fall frost. Sow seeds 0.25 to 0.5 inch (6.5–12.5 mm) deep, 8–12 inches (20.5–30.5 cm) apart, in rows 18–24 inches (45.5–61 cm) apart.

SPACE 8–12 inches (20.5–30.5 cm)

CARE Water moderately. Kale can survive freezing temperatures and becomes sweeter after the first frost.

HARVEST Harvest leaves after 55–75 days. Florets can also be eaten.

DISEASES/PESTS See cole crop pests and diseases (page 148).

VARIETIES/CULTIVARS Vates, winterbor, red Russian

POINT OF FACT Kale belongs to the same family as broccoli, and its flowers look like small broccoli florets. Kale helps with heart, bone, and skin health.

I GREW IT!

WHEN I GREW IT
DATE

NOTES

Kohlrabi

(Brassica oleracea var. gongylodes)

DESCRIPTION 6–18 inch (15–45.5 cm) tall plant with an edible, swollen, spherical stem and long-stemmed leaves

HARDY ZONES 2–10

PLANT Plant seeds 3–4 weeks before last frost date.

SPACE 5–8 inches (12.5–20.5 cm)

CARE Water moderately.

HARVEST Harvest stems 45–60 days after planting. Leaves and stems can be cooked as greens.

DISEASES/PESTS See cole crop pests and diseases (page 148).

VARIETIES/CULTIVARS Quickstar, purple Vienna, kossak

POINT OF FACT The name kohlrabi comes from the German words *kohl* (cabbage) and *rabi* (turnip), because it tastes like cabbage and looks like a turnip.

I GREW IT!

WHEN I GREW IT
DATE

NOTES

ANNUAL

Lettuce

(Lactuca sativa)

to

DESCRIPTION A 6–12 inch (15–30.5 cm) tall vegetable used in salads

HARDY ZONES 2–11

PLANT Plant seeds 2 weeks before the last frost date or in the fall, 8 weeks before the first frost.

SPACE 4–16 inches (10–40.5 cm)

CARE Water moderately. Lettuce prefers cool temperatures but cannot tolerate frost.

HARVEST Harvest loose leaf lettuce in 40 days, butterhead in 40–70 days, and romaine and iceberg in 80 days. Harvest outer leaves or cut the plant 1 inch (2.5 cm) above the soil level.

DISEASES/PESTS Spray aphids and pick off slugs or set a trap.

VARIETIES/CULTIVARS buttercrunch, salad bowl, red sails

POINT OF FACT The average American eats about 30 pounds (13.5 kg) of lettuce a year.

I GREW IT!

WHEN I GREW IT
DATE

NOTES

ANNUAL
Okra
(Abelmoschus esculentus)

DESCRIPTION 3–6 foot (1–2 m) tall plant with edible, spear-like pods

HARDY ZONES 2–11

PLANT Plant seeds 2–4 weeks after the last chance of frost in the spring.

SPACE 12–18 inches (30.5–45.5 cm)

CARE Water moderately.

HARVEST Harvest pods when they are 2–3 inches (5–7.5 cm) long, usually in 50–65 days.

DISEASES/PESTS Okra can be infected with verticillium and fusarium wilt. Remove affected plants. Spray insects with a blast of water to remove.

VARIETIES/CULTIVARS Clemson spineless, burgundy, jambalaya

POINT OF FACT Okra was grown by the ancient Egyptians and the Moors since about the 12th century BC. The word okra comes from a Western African language, possibly Igbo.

I GREW IT!

WHEN I GREW IT
DATE

NOTES

204

Onion

(Allium cepa)

DESCRIPTION 1–2 foot (30.5–61 cm) tall plant with an edible bulb growing underground

HARDY ZONES 2–10

PLANT Plant onion sets (small bulbs) in the spring.

SPACE 4–6 inches (10–15 cm)

CARE Water moderately.

HARVEST Harvest when the onion tops fall over and brown, usually after 100–120 days. To harvest, pull or dig the bulbs up from the ground, tops attached.

DISEASES/PESTS Onion diseases include fusarium bulb rot, smut, onion leaf blight, onion smudge, and downy mildew. Plant disease-resistant varieties.

VARIETIES/CULTIVARS Long-day varieties (better for cooler climates): Stuttgarter, yellow sweet Spanish, red wethersfield. Short-day varieties (better in warmer climates): white Bermuda

POINT OF FACT During the ancient Olympic Games, athletes would eat pounds of onions, believing them to promote strength.

◊ I GREW IT!

WHEN I GREW IT
DATE

NOTES

Parsnip
(Pastinaca sativa)

to

DESCRIPTION 3–foot (91 cm) tall vegetable grown for its edible taproot

HARDY ZONES 2–9

PLANT Plant seeds 2–3 weeks before the average last frost date.

SPACE 6–10 inches (15–25.5 cm)

CARE Water lightly.

HARVEST Harvest roots in 100–150 days, when the leaves reach 3 feet (91 cm) tall. The roots should be about 6–12 inches (15–30.5 cm) long. Dig them up with a spade.

DISEASES/PESTS Parsnips do not face any serious disease issues. Pests include swallowtail-butterfly caterpillars, which should be handpicked off, and root maggots, which can be discouraged by placing a 3–inch (7.5 cm) plastic square around the plant.

VARIETIES/CULTIVARS Avonresister, cobham improved marrow, gladiator

POINT OF FACT Sugar was a rarity in medieval Europe, so parsnip was used to sweeten and thicken puddings.

◊ I GREW IT!

WHEN I GREW IT
DATE

NOTES

ANNUAL

Peas

(Pisum sativum var. sativum, Pisum sativum var. saccharatum)

DESCRIPTION 1–1.5 foot (30.5–45.5 cm) tall plant grown for its peas or whole pods

HARDY ZONES 2–11

PLANT Plant seeds outdoors 4–6 weeks before the last frost. A second harvest can be planted 6–8 weeks before the first fall frost date.

SPACE 2 inches (5 cm)

CARE Water moderately.

HARVEST Harvest peas 60–70 days after planting. They are ready when they are sweet, thin-skinned, and tender.

DISEASES/PESTS Diseases include leaf spot, leaf scab, blight, rot, fusarium wilt, powdery mildew, botrytis, mold, damping off, and mosaic. Plant disease-resistant varieties. Hose off aphids and thrips.

VARIETIES/CULTIVARS Snowbird (snow pea), green arrow (garden pea)

POINT OF FACT Peas were domesticated in the Fertile Crescent about 11,000 years ago, making them one of the first crops. Wild peas were consumed even earlier. Neanderthals ate wild peas as early as 46,000 years ago.

I GREW IT!

WHEN I GREW IT
DATE

NOTES

Potato
(Solanum tuberosum)

DESCRIPTION 1–1.5 foot (30.5–45.5 cm) tall plant with large, edible tubers

HARDY ZONES 2–11

PLANT Plant seed potatoes (potato chunks with eyes) at various times depending on the type.

SPACE 12–14 inches (30.5–35.5 cm)

CARE Water moderately. Every 2 weeks, hill up the potatoes, adding soil so that only the stem is exposed.

HARVEST Harvest potatoes in 70–160 days, depending on the variety. Potatoes are ready to dig up after the flowers bloom on the plant.

DISEASES/PESTS Potato is affected by blight. Control blight with a spray of compost tea every 2 weeks. Control Colorado potato beetles, leafhoppers, and flea beetles with *Bacillus thuringiensis*. Spray aphids off with a hose.

VARIETIES/CULTIVARS Irish cobbler, Viking, elba

POINT OF FACT Potatoes were first domesticated in the Andes between 8,000 and 10,000 years ago. Potatoes and tomatoes are in the same family.

I GREW IT!

WHEN I GREW IT
DATE

NOTES

Pumpkin

(Cucurbita maxima, C. moschata, C. argyrosperma)

DESCRIPTION 10–12 feet (3–3.5 m) sprawling vine with large gourds eaten as a vegetable

HARDY ZONES 2–13

PLANT Plant seeds after the last frost.

SPACE 18–36 inches (45.5–91 cm)

CARE Water moderately to heavily. Side dress every 2 weeks. Prune the vines so that the plants can focus their energy on growing the fruit.

HARVEST Harvest pumpkins after 90–120 days. A mature pumpkin is a deep, solid color, and sounds hollow when tapped. Cut the fruit from the vine, leaving the stem attached.

DISEASES/PESTS Pumpkins can be infected by bacterial wilt, mosaic, and mildew. Plant disease resistant varieties. Spray cucumber beetles with neem. Spray off aphids with the hose.

VARIETIES/CULTIVARS Jack be Little (miniature), Autumn Gold (for carving), Dill's Atlantic Gold (giant), Sugar Treat (for pie)

POINT OF FACT The heaviest pumpkin to date weighed 2,624.6 pounds (1,190 kg).

WHEN I GREW IT
DATE

NOTES

Radicchio

(Cichorium intybus var. foliosum)

DESCRIPTION 4–6 inch (10–15 cm) tall plant with red and white leaves that are eaten as a salad green

HARDY ZONES 2–11

PLANT Plant seeds 2–3 weeks before the last frost or 8 weeks before the first frost.

SPACE 12 inches (30.5 cm)

CARE Water moderately. High temperatures will burn the leaves.

HARVEST Harvest heads in 60–65 days, cutting them slightly above soil level.

DISEASES/PESTS Pick off cabbage loopers and slugs; spray off aphids.

VARIETIES/CULTIVARS Chicory red verona, Augusto

POINT OF FACT Radicchio is common in Italian cuisine. *Radicchio* is the Italian term for all types of chicory, but in North America the word refers only to red-leafed varieties.

I GREW IT!

WHEN I GREW IT
DATE

NOTES

ANNUAL

Radish

(Raphanus sativus)

DESCRIPTION 2–3 foot (61–91 cm) tall root vegetable with edible roots, greens, and seedpods

HARDY ZONES 2–11

PLANT Plant seeds 4–6 weeks before the average last frost date and in the fall 4–6 weeks before the first frost.

SPACE 2 inches (5 cm)

CARE Water moderately.

HARVEST Harvest roots in 22–70 days, when they peek out of the soil. To harvest pods, allow the plant to flower and go to seed.

DISEASES/PESTS Radishes have no important disease issues. Spray insects off with the hose.

VARIETIES/CULTIVARS French breakfast, Burpee white

POINT OF FACT The ancient Greeks gave small gold radishes as an offering to the god Apollo.

I GREW IT!

WHEN I GREW IT
DATE

NOTES

211

PERENNIAL
Rhubarb
(Rheum rhabarbarum)

 to

DESCRIPTION 1–2 foot (30.5–61 cm) tall vegetable with edible reddish stalks most often used in desserts
NOTE: The leaves of the rhubarb are poisonous.

HARDY ZONES 2–6

PLANT Plant crowns as soon as the soil is workable in the spring.

SPACE 4 feet (1 m)

CARE Water moderately. Divide rhubarb every 2 years.

HARVEST Harvest stems in the second year of growth. Stems are ready when they are 12–18 inches (30.5–45.5 cm) long and red. They can be pulled off at the base.

DISEASES/PESTS Rhubarb is disease- and pest-resistant.

VARIETIES/CULTIVARS Crimson cherry, valentine, Canada red

POINT OF FACT While it is a vegetable, rhubarb is used as a fruit in jams and desserts.

I GREW IT!

WHEN I GREW IT
DATE

NOTES

212

Rutabaga
(Brassica napobrassica)

DESCRIPTION 1–2 feet (30.5–61 cm) tall vegetable with edible roots, leaves, and sprouts.

HARDY ZONES 3–9

PLANT Plant seeds 10–12 weeks before the first frost.

SPACE 8 inches (20.5 cm)

CARE Water moderately.

HARVEST Harvest rutabaga in 70–100 days, when the roots are 2–3 inches (5–7.5 cm) in diameter.

DISEASES/PESTS Aphids should be sprayed off, and flea beetles prevented with row covers.

VARIETIES/CULTIVARS American purple top, Laurentian

POINT OF FACT Before pumpkins, rutabagas were commonly used as jack-o'-lanterns.

WHEN I GREW IT
DATE

NOTES

Spinach
(Spinacia oleracea)

DESCRIPTION 6–12 inch (15–30.5 cm) tall plant grown for its edible leaves

HARDY ZONES 2–9

PLANT Plant seeds 4–6 weeks before the last frost.

SPACE 6–9 inches (15–23 cm)

CARE Water moderately.

HARVEST Harvest leaves in 35–50 days. Spinach bolts quickly and should be harvested as soon as it is ready.

DISEASES/PESTS Spray compost tea to prevent mildew and rust. Remove and destroy plants affected with mosaic. Spray aphids with water and prevent leaf miners by using row covers.

VARIETIES/CULTIVARS Giant nobel, Winter bloomsdale

POINT OF FACT Spinach is tolerant of cold weather and can survive temperatures as low as 15°F (-9°C). Spinach is a great source of vitamins A, B, and C.

I GREW IT!

WHEN I GREW IT
DATE

NOTES

Sweet Potato

(Ipomoea batatas)

DESCRIPTION A vine spreading up to 8–10 feet (2.5–3 m) and having edible tubers growing underground

HARDY ZONES 9–11, or as an annual

PLANT Plant slips (seedlings), 2 per 1.5-gallon (3.5 L) pot at a 45-degree angle. When the slips are 6–8 inches (15–20.5 cm) tall and after the last frost, plant them in the garden.

SPACE 12–18 inches (30.5–45.5 cm)

CARE Water moderately to heavily. Fertilize the plants 3–4 weeks after they are planted in the garden.

HARVEST Harvest sweet potatoes in about 100 days. Carefully dig up the tubers and sun-cure them for a few days.

DISEASES/PESTS Pests include flea beetles, which should be picked off by hand.

VARIETIES/CULTIVARS Beauregard, jewel, Vardaman

POINT OF FACT Sweet potatoes were domesticated in Central or South America more than 5,000 years ago. Sweet potatoes can be stored for as long as 6 months.

I GREW IT!

WHEN I GREW IT
DATE

NOTES

Swiss Chard

(Beta vulgaris var. vulgaris)

 to

DESCRIPTION 1–2 foot (30.5–61 cm) tall vegetable with edible, colorful stalks in reds, pinks, and yellows

HARDY ZONES 2–11

PLANT Plant seeds 2–3 weeks before the last frost.

SPACE 6–8 inches (15–20.5 cm)

CARE Water moderately to heavily.

HARVEST Baby leaves are ready for harvest after about 30 days, while mature leaves are ready in 45–60 days. For best flavor, harvest leaves when they are no more than 12 inches (30.5 cm) long.

DISEASES/PESTS Spray off aphids with water, and remove leaves infested with leaf miner eggs.

VARIETIES/CULTIVARS Lucullus, ruby red, bright lights

POINT OF FACT Swiss chard was domesticated 2,000 years ago in the Mediterranean region. It was likely developed from a species of wild beet.

I GREW IT!

WHEN I GREW IT
DATE

NOTES

Tomato
(Lycopersicon esculentum)

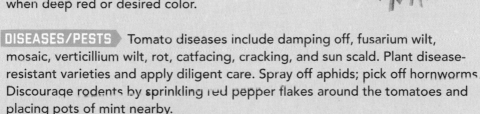

DESCRIPTION 3–6 foot (1–2 m) tall plant with edible fruit

HARDY ZONES 10–11, or as an annual

PLANT Plant seedlings after the last frost or start tomato seeds indoors.

SPACE 3 feet (91 cm)

CARE Water moderately until they fruit, and then heavily. Side dress weekly once they begin to fruit.

HARVEST Harvest tomatoes after 60–80 days, when deep red or desired color.

DISEASES/PESTS Tomato diseases include damping off, fusarium wilt, mosaic, verticillium wilt, rot, catfacing, cracking, and sun scald. Plant disease-resistant varieties and apply diligent care. Spray off aphids; pick off hornworms. Discourage rodents by sprinkling red pepper flakes around the tomatoes and placing pots of mint nearby.

VARIETIES/CULTIVARS Early varieties, 60 or fewer days to harvest: Early cascade, early girl. Mid-season varieties, 70–80 days: floramerica, fantastic. Late-season varieties, 80 days or more: Amish paste, brandywine. Cherry tomatoes: Matt's wild cherry, sun gold.

POINT OF FACT Though today a staple in Italian cuisine, the tomato was not introduced to Italy until the 16th century.

I GREW IT!

WHEN I GREW IT
DATE

NOTES

217

Turnip
(Brassica rapa)

DESCRIPTION 6–12 inch (15–30.5 cm) tall vegetable grown for its bright purple root

HARDY ZONES 2–9

PLANT Plant seeds 2–3 weeks after the last frost and again in late summer.

SPACE 4–6 inches (10–15 cm)

CARE Water moderately.

HARVEST Harvest turnips 45–60 days after planting.

DISEASES/PESTS Pick off or spray off insects.

VARIETIES/CULTIVARS Just right, yellow globe, purple top white globe

POINT OF FACT Turnips have been grown for more than 3,000 years. Young turnips taste better than older ones, which become bitter.

I GREW IT!

WHEN I GREW IT
DATE

NOTES

ANNUAL

Zucchini

(Cucurbita pepo)

DESCRIPTION 1–2.5 foot (30.5–76 cm) tall fruiting plant

HARDY ZONES 2–11

PLANT Plant seeds from spring to midsummer.

SPACE 24 inches (61 cm)

CARE Water moderately. Fertilize after blooms appear.

HARVEST Harvest fruit 60 days after planting when it is about 6–8 inches (15–20.5 cm).

DISEASES/PESTS Squash vine borers can be prevented with row covers, stink bugs and cucumber beetles should be picked off, and aphids should be sprayed with water.

VARIETIES/CULTIVARS Goldbar, cocozelle

POINT OF FACT Pumpkin and zucchini originated from the same plant, which was eaten as long ago as 10,000 years.

WHEN I GREW IT
DATE

NOTES

PART IV

FRUITS
AND
NUTS

N. DAWSON

Your family has moved from an apart-ment to a house with a big backyard! You have some exploring to do. There are elderberries growing along the fence line, and a pecan and apple tree. Come harvest time, it will be good eating. Especially that apple pie! Come late summer, the elderberries turn purple and you harvest them for a pie. In the fall, the pecans fall and you bake a pecan pie. But there are still no apples! *What would you do?*

CHAPTER 1

Soft Fruits

Soft fruit refers to fruit with soft, edible skin, but no pit. It's what you might think of as a berry. *Soft fruit* is used in place of *berry* because berry is a scientific term meaning a fleshy, stoneless fruit from a single flower and ovary. Scientifically, a grape is a berry, but so is a banana and an eggplant. Meanwhile, neither a strawberry nor a raspberry qualifies as a true berry.

GRAPES

RASPBERRIES

Most soft fruit grows on vines, bushes, or brambles. Exceptions are the mulberry, a native soft fruit that grows on tall trees, and strawberries, which grow on the ground. You're unlikely to plant a mulberry tree as part of a small garden, but you may inherit one. If so, you're in luck, because it requires no care and produces a large harvest each spring.

Fruit vs. Veggies

Growing vegetables and growing fruit are as different as night and day. Most vegetables are grown as small annual plants, whereas most fruit grows on bushes, vines, or trees—garden fixtures that live for years. In fact, you may have inherited a fruit tree planted by a previous homeowner. It may even have been planted in the wild by a bird or squirrel! Though fruit plants are longer-lived, they require little care once they mature. Simply let them be. Or increase the amount of fruit by pruning in late winter and adding fertilizer and mulch in the spring. Then reap the harvest.

Strawberries

Strawberries are unusual among fruits because they grow on tender, low-to-the-ground plants. All varieties have been culti-vated from the tiny wild strawberries that originated in North America and still grow wild today. They are perennials that sprout in early spring—inconvenient timing as they are sensitive to frost and must be covered in blankets if the temperature dips below freezing. On the plus side, they produce in June—before most other fruits. If you live in a cooler climate, you can purchase everbearing plants. These plants produce strawberries from June to early fall but do not like hot summers!

TRY IT → Grow Strawberries

You can grow strawberries in a patch, in a container, or under trees as ground cover. The traditional way is in a patch with straw used as mulch (hence the name strawberries).

> **WHAT YOU'LL NEED**
>
> ➢ three or more strawberry seedlings, 3x5 feet (91x152 cm) in-ground or raised garden bed, compost or manure, straw, garden fork or shovel, and a trowel or spoon

STEP 1 Prepare your garden bed by working compost or manure into the soil.

STEP 2 Plant a seedling every 15 inches (38 cm) in the center of the garden lengthwise. Plant so that the entire root ball is beneath the soil.

STEP 3 Add straw around the strawberry plants to cover the soil. This will prevent weeds, and the straw will add nutrients as it rots.

STEP 4 Water after planting and continue to water moderately throughout the growing season.

STEP 5 For June-bearing plants: The first year, it's best for the plants if no strawberries grow. Pick off all white flowers as they bloom. For everbearing plants, disallow June strawberries by picking off flowers, but allow later flowers to bloom into strawberries.

STEP 6 When the ground begins to freeze, cut the plants down to 1 inch (2.5 cm) and cover them with 4 inches (10 cm) of straw or pine needles to protect them from frost.

STEP 7 Uncover the plants in early spring—when the temperature is unlikely to dip below 20°F (-7°C).

STEP 8 If a frost is expected, cover the new plants with blankets or sheets.

STEP 9 Harvest the strawberries in June, and for everbearing varieties, later in the season, when they are red and ripe.

I DID IT! DATE:

Fruit Brambles and Bushes

Plants are full of surprises that make sense upon a closer look. Raspberries, blackberries, and their kin are members of the rose family. In the wild, they have the thorns to prove it, though these have been bred out of many garden varieties. Hybrids include loganberries, tayberries, boysenberries, and others. They are grown in basically the same way—several feet apart tied to stakes for support. Brambles spread through their roots. To keep them under control, either plant in containers or with grass surrounding their patch. Mowing will keep unwanted

CLIMBING ROSE

shoots under control. Dead canes (branches) should be cut back each year or you will soon have a tangled, thorny mess.

Fruit bushes include currants, cranberries, cape gooseberries, and blueberries. Just as the raspberry is related to the rose, the blueberry is cousins with the azalea. Both love acidic soil and are ideal for growing in containers. With proper care, a blueberry bush will last 20 years!

GOOSEBERRY

RED CURRANT

BLACK CURRANT

MOUNTAIN CURRANT

Anatomy of Fruit Brambles and Bushes

BRAMBLE A thorny, viny shrub.

CANE The branches that grow from the roots of brambles.

SOFT FRUIT A small fruit with soft skin and no pit. It is often thought of as a berry.

PIT The hard center of some fruits.

TRY IT →

Grow a Blueberry Bush in a Container

STEP 1 Fill the container with potting mix, leaving 3 inches (7.5 cm) at the top.

STEP 2 Bury the root ball.

STEP 3 Water moderately, remembering that plants in containers need more water than those in the ground.

STEP 4 Blueberries can survive cold winters if planted in the ground. But plants in containers aren't as well insulated. Move your blueberries to a basement or garage before the first frost.

I DID IT! DATE:

BLUEBERRY BUSH

Can Berries

The purpose of canning is to stop bacterial growth. Some canning requires both heat and pressure to keep bacteria out. But fruits that are  high in acid need only heat. In a process called water bath canning, you will pack fruit into airtight jars and boil them in a large pot.

> **WHAT YOU'LL NEED**
>
> ➤ a large pot; a jar rack; 4-quart (3.5 L) jars; heat-resistant gloves; berry juice (optional); and 7 pounds (3 kg) of berries (Note: Strawberries do not can well.)

STEP 1 Place the open jars in the rack and sterilize them by boiling.

STEP 2 Fill the jars evenly with raw berries.

STEP 3 Boil water or juice and pour it over the fruit to cover.

STEP 4 Working carefully, because the jars will now be hot, seal the jars with the lids.

STEP 5 Place the rack in boiling water again for 15 minutes. Remove and cool.

STEP 6 Store in the pantry.

I DID IT! DATE:

Grow These Unusual Fruits

HARDY KIWI

FINGER LIME

HONEYBERRY

CAPE GOOSEBERRY

GOJI BERRY

CHOKE BERRY

HARDY PASSION FRUIT

Fruit Vines

Two fruits that grow on vines are grapes and kiwi. Grapes can be grown from zones 4 to 10. The main care involved is providing scaffolding and pruning. Grow grapes on an arbor or fence. Remove all flowers and grapes the first two years or they will weigh down and break the young vines. In the winter, prune the vine about 80 percent. The third year, you will begin to have grapes you can harvest.

The fuzzy kiwi you find in the store is a subtropical fruit. In zones 7 and higher, try growing hardy kiwi, a smaller fruit with thinner skin. This fruit also requires even more patience than grapes—it may be seven years before fruit grows on the vine. You need lots of space—vines can grow 28 feet (8.5 m) long!

Berry Good Pie

Do you have berries growing in your yard? Careful! Many berries are highly poisonous. But others are edible. You may not be familiar with these edible berries because they don't travel well and thus aren't for sale in the grocery store. But if they're growing in your yard, why not bake them in a pie?

ELDERBERRY Eaten raw, these will give you a bellyache, but baked in a pie, they make a sweet treat. They grow on bushes with delicate white flowers that bloom into deep purple berries. Pair them with rhubarb for a perfect mix of sweet and sour.

MULBERRY Mulberries look like blackberries, except instead of low brambles, they grow on trees so tall that handpicking is impossible. They are native to North America and are considered by some to be a nuisance because of their staining berries that fall here and there. But look on the bright side! Mulberries provide free fruit that cannot be found in the store. In early summer, lay down a tarp and gather them as they fall. They can be eaten raw but are best baked in a pie.

Beware These Berries!

These common weeds have poisonous berries:

POKEWEED Its red stalk can grow 10 feet (3 m) tall, though it's usually pulled up before then because the plant is a weed with no real uses. Poisonous purple berries grow in clusters.

BELLADONNA A relative of eggplant, they resemble each other, but belladonna grows in the wild. Purple bell-shaped flowers give way to purple berries that are among the most poisonous in the world.

TRACK IT ↘ Berry Spotting

Draw a picture of any berries you have growing in your yard or nearby. Using the information above and native plant websites, try to identify them. (Remember, only eat berries if you are sure of what they are!)

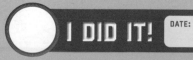

I DID IT! DATE:

Native Fruits

PAWPAW
Grow zones 5–8

WILD GRAPES
Grow zones 2–10

ELDERBERRY
Grow zones 3–8

BLUEBERRY
Grow zones 3–10

CRANBERRY
Grow zones 3–8

MULBERRY
Grow zones 4–8

CHAPTER 2

Fruit and Nut Trees

Trees are grown for their stateliness, shade, and sometimes for their fruit and nuts. Many sweet fruits grow on trees. And so do many nuts. A true nut is a hardened fruit that contains a single seed within. In the case of chestnuts and hazelnuts, we eat these seeds. In the case of acorns, we do not. Though many nuts are not true nuts but a hard part of another type of fruit, we think of them all as nuts because they are hard parts of plants that we tend to roast, salt, and eat.

Fruit and nut trees can be divided into three categories: hardy trees, subtropical trees, and tropical trees. Hardy trees can be grown in parts of the country with cold winters. Some, but not all, require chilly temperatures to thrive. They include apple, pear, plum, cherry, and pawpaw trees. Peaches, nectarines, and apricots can also withstand cold winters, but their buds may suffer during an early frost. They also need very hot summers. For this reason, they are commonly grown in zones 5–9. Subtropical trees can be grown in zones 8–10. They include most citrus fruits. Tropical fruit trees, like banana, breadfruit, and mango trees, must be grown in zones 11–12. In the United States, that limits them to Puerto Rico and Hawaii. There, they are likely something you inherit rather than plant in a garden because of the time it takes them to mature and their towering height. Likewise, most nut trees are tall and long-lived. With many native to North America, you may find one growing nearby. With space being a challenge for growing trees, one solution is to plant smaller or columnar varieties, and many fruit trees, have dwarf varieties.

Apple and Pear Trees

Apple and pear trees are grown in the same way. However, apple trees are more versatile. They can be grown in all fifty states so long as you choose the right variety. Most apple trees are not self-pollinating, so you'll need to plant two trees for them to bear fruit. Apples are categorized as dessert if they are best eaten raw, and cooking if they are best baked. You can choose one of each, though they must bloom at the same time for cross-pollination. For a garden, you'll likely choose a dwarf variety. Even many orchards opt for dwarf varieties nowadays so that the trees can be grown closer together and the apples can be picked without a ladder.

A final consideration is the shape of the tree. Apples can be grown as trees, espaliers, or columns. Espalier apple trees grow flat along a wall or other structure. Columnar trees grow in a straight line, with no branches. Either shape takes up less space than a tree. Columnar trees spread to just 3 feet (91 cm) and can easily be grown in a pot on the patio.

How Many Apples?

The number of apples a tree produces annually depends on its size.

Height (feet)

DWARF
1–6 bushels

SEMI-DWARF
4–10 bushels

STANDARD
8–18 bushels

1 bushel = 40–42 pounds (18–19 kg) =
80–84 large, 120–126 medium, or 160–168 small apples

TRACK IT ↘ Make an Apple Chart

To determine which two apple trees to grow, make a chart. To cross-pollinate, the trees need to have the same bloom time. Whether you choose dessert or cooking apples depends on your preference: snacking (dessert), baking (cooking), or both/one of each. Finally, size and shape refers to whether dwarf, columnar, or espalier varieties are even available.

Apples that Grow in My Grow Zone

Apple Type	Bloom Time	Dessert, Cooking, or Both	Size and Shape

I DID IT! DATE:

WHAT YOU'LL NEED

≫ a shovel, garden soil, mulch, and two dwarf apple trees

STEP 1 Dig two holes at least 10 feet (3 m) apart but no more than 20 feet (6 m) apart. Each hole should be 2 feet (61 cm) deep and twice as wide as the root ball.

STEP 2 Set the root balls in the holes and fill the holes with the garden soil.

STEP 3 Cover the soil with mulch.

STEP 4 Water the young tree every few days unless it rains.

STEP 5 The dwarf apple trees will begin producing fruit in 2–4 years. In the spring, lots of little apples will drop. Don't worry. More will grow.

STEP 6 Apples are ready to pick when they are their desired color and size and can easily be pulled from the tree by twisting them.

NOTE: To grow in a container, plant the tree in a pot slightly wider than the root ball. Fill the gap with potting mix. Pot up each year.

I DID IT! DATE:

Other Hardy Fruit Trees

Cherry trees double as decorative floral trees and easy-to-grow fruit trees. Note that sweet cherry trees are larger, grow in zones 5–8, and can be either self-pollinating or not, whereas sour cherry trees (for baking) grow in zones 4–7, are smaller, and are always self-pollinating. To grow a cherry tree, simply plant it and water during droughts. You will get a small number of cherries the first few years, but soon, you'll have more than enough. Birds love cherries, so you'll either need to cast a net over the tree or agree to share.

SWEET CHERRY

Plum trees have many varieties. The main categories are Japanese, European, Damson, and Wild (to North America). They can be sweet or tart, and most are available in dwarf varieties.

Peaches, nectarines, and apricots are all grown basically the same way. They prefer dry, sandy soil, but can be grown in other soil types. They are susceptible to spring frosts as they are early bloomers. You can protect them with a blanket if the temperature is expected to drop.

PEACH

The tree looks tropical and the fruit tastes tropical. (Imagine a cross between a banana, mango, and lemon.) But the pawpaw tree grows in zones 5–9. Native to North America, it is easy to grow and care for.

PAWPAW

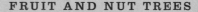

Types of Young Trees

Trees are usually sold as bare root (no soil attached to their roots). These must be planted as soon as they arrive.

They can also be sold as root ball (roots in soil). Check to make sure the plant isn't root-bound, meaning the roots are growing in a circle along the inside of the container.

Tree age (size and branches) will vary by species.

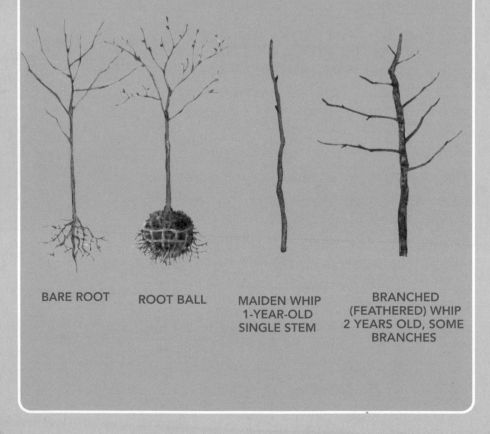

BARE ROOT

ROOT BALL

MAIDEN WHIP
1-YEAR-OLD
SINGLE STEM

BRANCHED
(FEATHERED) WHIP
2 YEARS OLD, SOME
BRANCHES

TRY IT →  Prune a Fruit Tree

Most fruit trees should be pruned in late winter when they are dormant. Stone fruit trees (such as peaches) should be pruned after buds form.

> **WHAT YOU'LL NEED**
>
> ➢ snips for smallest branches, lopper for medium branches, saw for largest branches, and pruning shears to prune branches that are dead, damaged, or diseased

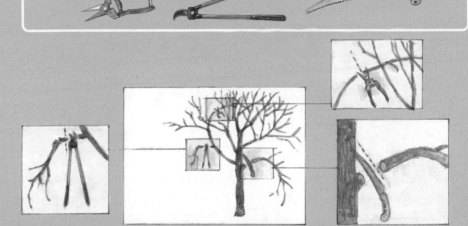

If two branches are touching or crossing, trim one of them.

WHERE TO TRIM

Cut branches just above a healthy bud or branch/twig, or, to remove the whole branch, at the base of a branch. But leave the collar—the thick part of where the branch meets the tree—to prevent disease.

HOW TO TRIM

Trim diagonally so that the cut is level to the next branch or the trunk. This allows rainwater to run off so that the cut can dry and heal.

 **I DID IT!** DATE:

How to Spot Dead, Damaged, or Diseased Branches

The following are signs of an unhealthy branch:

1. The leaves on that branch are dead, whereas the leaves on the rest of the tree are still green.

2. The bark is discolored.

3. The branch is oozing sap.

4. The branch is broken.

5. When in doubt, scrape the bark away from a small section. The wood beneath the bark should be brown and hard rather than greenish and soft.

Citrus Fruit Trees

Citrus fruit trees are beautiful and fragrant, and available in dwarf varieties. They prefer a temperature of 60°F (16°C) and warmer, with 60–70 percent humidity, so grow zone 10 in Southern California and Florida are ideal for them. However, some varieties are adapted to much lower humidity and can be grown in the hot deserts of the Southwest. You can also try growing a citrus tree in a container and move it to a sunny indoor spot for the winter.

ORANGES, LEMONS, LIMES, GRAPEFRUIT, POMELOS, CITRON, MANDARIN ORANGES, TANGERINES, CLEMENTINES, KUMQUATS

TRACK IT ↘   Identify Nut Trees

Many nut trees are native to America. You may have one growing near you. Which kind is it? Look at the illustrations and mark which ones you see nearby. Add any others not listed, too.

    NOTE: Horse chestnuts are poisonous. Though unrelated to other chestnut trees, and having different looking nuts, they are sometimes confused with chestnut trees because of their name.

☐ Chestnut   ☐ Walnut   ☐ Other

☐ Pine Nut   ☐ Black Walnut

☐ Hickory

I DID IT!   DATE:

TAKE IT TO THE NEXT LEVEL ↗

Harvest Nuts from Native Trees

Do you or a neighbor have a nut tree growing in your yard? Why not harvest and use the nuts?

STEP 1 ▸ Gather the nuts as soon as they fall or can be shaken off the tree.

STEP 2 ▸ Place in a single layer in your attic, garage, or other dry space.

STEP 3 ▸ Turn each week.

STEP 4 ▸ When they are dry, use a nutcracker or hammer to break them open. Remove the nut meat and eat raw or roasted.

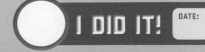

I DID IT!   DATE:

FRUIT AND NUT GUIDE

Most fruits and nuts grow on trees and long-lasting shrubs. That means they require more space, but you can harvest them every year. You may even have a fruit or nut tree on your property already!

LIGHT NEEDS

Full sun

Partial sun

Partial shade

Full shade

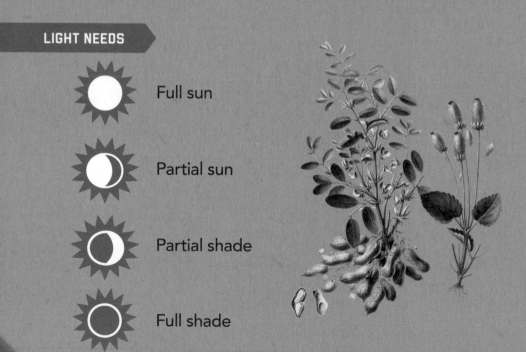

ELBERTA PEACH

Almond Tree
(Prunus dulcis)

DESCRIPTION 13–30 foot (4–9 m) tree with skinny green leaves and almond pod clusters

HARDY ZONES 5–8

PLANT Plant sapling in the spring. Wet roots before planting, spread the roots to prevent matting, and do not bend the main taproot. Plant the tree as far down as the color difference on the roots and trunk.

SPACE 15–20 feet (4.5–6 m)

CARE Water moderately. Paint the bottom of the trunk with white latex paint or wrap the trunk with 4 inches (10 cm) of tree guard to prevent rodent injury and sun scald.

HARVEST Harvest after 2–4 years, in late August through September. Gather fallen nuts and dry them in the sun for 2–3 days.

DISEASES/PESTS Control diseases with specialized citrus and nut orchard sprays. Rake out tent caterpillar webs.

VARIETIES/CULTIVARS Dwarf: All-in-one; Full-size: Hall's hardy

POINT OF FACT Chocolate makers use 40 percent of the world's almonds.

I GREW IT!

WHEN I GREW IT
DATE

NOTES

248

PERENNIAL VINE

American Cranberry

(Vaccinium macrocarpon)

DESCRIPTION Low, creeping vine up to 7 feet (2 m) long and 2–8 inches (5–20 cm) tall

HARDY ZONES 2–7

PLANT Plant young vines in the spring.

SPACE 2–3 feet (61–91 cm)

CARE Water moderately.

HARVEST Harvest September–October after 2–3 years.

DISEASES/PESTS Spray aphids off with water, trap whiteflies.

VARIETIES/CULTIVARS Thunder lake

POINT OF FACT Cranberries were first commercially cultivated around 1816 on Cape Cod. Commercial growers harvest the fruit by filling a bog with water, churning the water to loosen the berries, and allowing them to float to the top.

I GREW IT!

WHEN I GREW IT
DATE

NOTES

American Elderberry/ Canada Elderberry

(Sambucus canadensis)

DESCRIPTION 5–12 foot (1.5–3.5 m) tall and wide shrubs

HARDY ZONES 3–8

PLANT Plant young shrubs in the spring.

SPACE 6–8 feet (2–2.5 m)

CARE Water moderately. Side dress young plants in the spring.

HARVEST Harvest berries in the summer, when they are dark purple.

DISEASES/PESTS Prune canes infested by diseases or cane borers.

VARIANTS/CULTIVARS European elderberry

POINT OF FACT When baked, elderberries are very sweet, so it's best to complement them with a sour component such as lemon or rhubarb.

I GREW IT!

WHEN I GREW IT
DATE

NOTES

Apple Tree
(Malus domestica)

DESCRIPTION 8–40 foot (2.5–12 m) fruit tree

HARDY ZONES 2–10

PLANT Plant 2 compatible saplings in spring or fall.

SPACE 15–18 feet (4.5–5.5 m) for full-size trees; 4–8 feet (1–2.5 m) for dwarf trees

CARE Water moderately. Prune mature trees annually.

HARVEST Harvest from August to October, when apples are their desired color.

DISEASES/PESTS Apples are prone to many diseases and insects. Use pesticides or an anti-insect oil. Consider planting disease-resistant varieties such as Prima, Priscilla, Liberty, and Freedom.

VARIETIES/CULTIVARS Gala, golden delicious, McIntosh red, Cortland, honey crisp, Fuji, Granny Smith, red delicious, Jonagold

POINT OF FACT An overripe apple can still be used for cooking. March 11 is Johnny Appleseed Day.

I GREW IT!

WHEN I GREW IT
DATE

NOTES

....

Apricot Tree

(Prunus armeniaca)

DESCRIPTION A small tree that has white flowers and is semi self-fruiting

HARDY ZONES 5–8

PLANT Plant sapling in a hole deep enough for the roots. Note: To encourage fruiting, it is best to plant a pair.

SPACE 20 feet (6 m) for full-size trees and 15 feet (4.5 m) for semi-dwarf trees

CARE Water moderately.

HARVEST Harvest in June–August. They will start bearing fruit in 2–5 years.

DISEASES/PESTS Plant disease-resistant varieties. Control pests with neem oil or fruit and nut orchard spray.

VARIETIES/CULTIVARS Apium, August glo, Autumn royal, Blenheim, Chinese (Mormon), earligold, floragold, garden Annie, gold kist

POINT OF FACT Dried apricots are a great source of iron.

I GREW IT!

WHEN I GREW IT
DATE

NOTES

Avocado Tree

(Persea americana)

DESCRIPTION 30–40 foot (9–12 m) tall tree that grows avocados

HARDY ZONES 9–11

PLANT Plant saplings in a container or in the ground.

SPACE 20–30 feet (6–9 m)

CARE Water moderately.

HARVEST Harvest after 3–4 years, in February–September. Pick the fruit when it is still unripe.

DISEASES/PESTS Root rot and anthracnose

VARIETIES/CULTIVARS Lamb hass, shapard, reed, wurtz, hass

POINT OF FACT Avocados contain monosaturated fat, known as the "good fat." Avocado ice cream is a popular dessert in Brazil.

I GREW IT!

WHEN I GREW IT
DATE

NOTES

253

Banana and Plantain
(Musa)

DESCRIPTION A genus of plants 4–25 feet (1–7.5 m) tall with palmlike leaves and bananas or plantains growing in bunches

HARDY ZONES 9–10

PLANT Plant young plants in a sunny place in a hole large enough to accommodate the root system.

SPACE 6–25 feet (2–7.5 m)

CARE Water moderately. Side dress once a month.

HARVEST Harvest 15–18 months after planting, when bananas are fully grown, but still green.

DISEASES/PESTS Consult extension.

VARIETIES/CULTIVARS cavendish, Enano gigante, high color mini

POINT OF FACT Though tall, banana plants are not trees, having no woody parts. Banana leaves are large and flexible and can be used as eco-friendly plates.

 **I GREW IT!**

WHEN I GREW IT
DATE

NOTES

Blackberries
(Rubus fruticosus)

DESCRIPTION A bush or cane that produces fruit

HARDY ZONES 4–10

PLANT Plant young bushes or canes in late fall or early spring in a container or the ground.

SPACE 3 feet (91 cm)

CARE Water moderately. Cut away dead canes every 1 or 2 years to avoid overgrowth. Side dress each spring.

HARVEST Harvest fully black berries between July and August.

DISEASES/PESTS Remove raspberry borers, and destroy infested parts of the plant.

VARIETIES/CULTIVARS Arapaho, black satin, Cheyenne

POINT OF FACT Blackberries will not ripen after they are picked.

 **I GREW IT!**

WHEN I GREW IT
DATE

NOTES

SHRUB
Blueberries
(Cyanococcus)

DESCRIPTION 6–12 foot (2–3.5 m) tall fruit bushes

HARDY ZONES 3–7

PLANT Plant young bushes in early spring in a container or raised bed filled with acidic soil. It's best to plant more than 1 for cross-pollination.

SPACE 4–5 feet (1–1.5 m)

CARE Water heavily. Side dress each spring with 10-10-10 fertilizer.

HARVEST Harvest from June to August when the blueberries can be easily pulled off the stem.

DISEASES/PESTS Plant disease-resistant varieties and use a bird net to keep birds away.

VARIETIES/CULTIVARS Highbush, lowbush, rabbiteye

POINT OF FACT In spring, the bushes have white blossoms, in summer, ripe berries, and in fall, red leaves, making them decorative as well as useful.

I GREW IT!

WHEN I GREW IT
DATE

NOTES

TREE

Breadfruit

(Artocarpus altilis)

DESCRIPTION 40–60 foot (12–18 m) tall fruit tree

HARDY ZONES 9–11

PLANT Plant a root shoot in a container to be transplanted after 3–5 months.

SPACE 40 feet (12 m)

CARE Water heavily when young, moderately once established.

HARVEST Harvest after 2–3 years; the tree will start to bear fruit.

DISEASES/PESTS Manage pests such as mealybugs, soft scale, and ants with sprays or oils.

POINT OF FACT Polynesian settlers brought breadfruit to Hawaii, where it is known as ulu. When cooked, breadfruit smells like freshly baked bread.

I GREW IT!

WHEN I GREW IT
DATE

NOTES

Cherry Tree

(Prunus avium—sweet and Prunus cerasus—sour)

DESCRIPTION 35-foot (10.5 m) tall (for sweet cherries) or 20-foot (6 m) tall (for sour cherries) tree with small stone fruit

HARDY ZONES 4–8

PLANT Plant sapling in the spring. Sweet cherry trees may require a second tree for pollination, whereas sour cherry trees are self-pollinating.

SPACE 5–40 feet (1.5–12 m) depending on the variety

CARE Water moderately.

HARVEST Harvest in early June through late July after 2 or 3 years.

DISEASES/PESTS Control insects such as Japanese beetles with sprays or oil; deter birds with netting.

VARIETIES/CULTIVARS
Sweet: Black tartarian, bing, Stella
Sour: Montmorency

POINT OF FACT Cherry blossoms are Japan's national flower. In Washington, DC, the annual Cherry Blossom Festival commemorates the 1912 gift of 3,000 trees from the mayor of Tokyo to the United States.

I GREW IT!

WHEN I GREW IT
DATE

NOTES

SHRUB
Chokeberry
(Aronia)

DESCRIPTION A genus of 3–6 foot (1–1.5 m) tall fruit shrubs

HARDY ZONES 3–8

PLANT Plant young bushes in acidic soil in the spring.

SPACE 7–10 feet (2–3 m)

CARE Water moderately. Prune every few years.

HARVEST Harvest summer to winter when berries are completely ripe.

DISEASES/PESTS Control insects with sprays or oils. Aphids can be sprayed off with water.

VARIETIES/CULTIVARS Autumn magic, nero, Viking

POINT OF FACT The chokeberry is a member of the rose family.

 **I GREW IT!**

WHEN I GREW IT
DATE

NOTES

Crabapple
(Malus sylvestris)

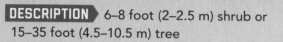

DESCRIPTION 6–8 foot (2–2.5 m) shrub or 15–35 foot (4.5–10.5 m) tree

HARDY ZONES 4–8

PLANT Plant sapling in the spring or fall.

SPACE 10–25 feet apart (3–7.5 m)

CARE Water heavily when young, then moderately.

HARVEST Harvest summer–fall, when the fruit is fully grown.

DISEASES/PESTS Prune branches infected by diseases such as Botrysphaeria canker, fire blight, and frogeye leaf spot.

VARIETIES/CULTIVARS jewelberry, coralburst, strawberry parfait

POINT OF FACT Crabapples taste overly tart raw but can be baked into desserts the same as other apples. Crabapples are high in pectin, making them ideal for jelly and jam making.

I GREW IT!

WHEN I GREW IT

DATE

NOTES

TREE
European Pear
(Pyrus communis)

DESCRIPTION 8–40 foot (2–12 m) tall fruit tree

HARDY ZONES 5–8

PLANT Plant saplings in late winter or early spring. Two are needed for cross-pollination.

SPACE 8–20 feet (2–6 m)

CARE Water moderately.

HARVEST Harvest August–October. Pick when not yet ripe and allow to ripen off the tree.

DISEASES/PESTS Pick off pests and destroy.

VARIETIES/CULTIVARS anjou, bartlett forelle

POINT OF FACT There are over 3,000 varieties of pears worldwide. China is the world's largest pear producer.

 **I GREW IT!**

WHEN I GREW IT
DATE

NOTES

Fig Tree
(Ficus carica)

DESCRIPTION 10–30 foot (3–9 m) tall fruit tree

HARDY ZONES 7–11

PLANT Plant a sapling in a pot or the ground in the spring.

SPACE 10–30 feet (3–9 m)

CARE Water moderately.

HARVEST Harvest spring–fall when fully ripe.

DISEASES/PESTS Prune diseased branches; use insecticidal soap on scale and mealybugs.

VARIETIES/CULTIVARS Celestial, black jack, yellow longneck

POINT OF FACT Fig trees have no blossoms on their branches because they blossom inside the fruit. Ever heard a grown-up call Newtons "Fig Newtons"? After more than 100 years as Fig Newtons, "fig" was dropped from the cookie's name in 2012.

I GREW IT!

WHEN I GREW IT
DATE

NOTES

Finger Lime
(Citrus australasica)

to

DESCRIPTION 10–20 foot (3–6 m) tall fruit tree with thorns

HARDY ZONES 10–11, or in a container

PLANT Plant a sapling in the ground or in a container.

SPACE 10–20 feet (3–6 m)

CARE Water moderately.

HARVEST Harvest year-round, when the fruit easily pulls off the branches.

DISEASES/PESTS Remove any dying or diseased branches.

VARIETIES/CULTIVARS alstonville, byron sunrise, collette

POINT OF FACT Finger limes are native to Australia, where they have been eaten for thousands of years. A nickname is citrus caviar because the fruit is filled with bright citrus-flavored beads that look like fish eggs.

◖ I GREW IT! ▷

WHEN I GREW IT
DATE

NOTES

263

Goji Berry Tree

(Lycium barbarum or *Lycium chinense)*

DESCRIPTION Thorny shrub 3–6 feet (1–2 m) tall

HARDY ZONES 5–9

PLANT Plant sapling in a pot or in the ground.

SPACE 1–2 feet (30.5–61 cm)

CARE Water heavily. Prune after the second year.

HARVEST Harvest summer–fall, when berries are fully ripe.

DISEASES/PESTS Deter birds with netting.

POINT OF FACT Dried goji berries are eaten like raisins. They are also known as wolfberries.

I GREW IT!

WHEN I GREW IT
DATE

NOTES

Gooseberry

(Ribes uva-crispa)

DESCRIPTION 3–5 foot (1–1.5 m) tall scraggly fruit bush

HARDY ZONES 3–5

PLANT Plant sapling in the fall.

SPACE 3–6 feet (1–2 m)

CARE Water moderately. Side dress in spring with a nitrogen-high fertilizer.

HARVEST Harvest 3 years after planting, in June–July, when berries are ripe.

DISEASES/PESTS Remove diseased branches; address pests with orchard spray.

VARIETIES/CULTIVARS invicta, Hinnonmaki red, captivator

POINT OF FACT One gooseberry bush can yield 8–10 pounds of fruit per season. It belongs to the same family as the currant.

WHEN I GREW IT
DATE

NOTES

....

265

PERENNIAL VINE

Grape
(Vitis)

DESCRIPTION Genus of fruit-bearing vines

HARDY ZONES 5–9

PLANT Plant young plants in the ground under supports on which they can grow.

SPACE 6–10 feet (2–3 m)

CARE Water moderately. Side dress once a month.

HARVEST Harvest in summer beginning in the third season.

DISEASES/PESTS Prune diseased branches.

VARIETIES/CULTIVARS Canadice, himrod

POINT OF FACT Grape seeds contain oils used in the manufacture of skin care products. Wild grapes have smaller fruit than domesticated grapes and may or may not be sweet.

I GREW IT!

WHEN I GREW IT
DATE

NOTES

TREE

Grapefruit
(Citrus x paradisi)

DESCRIPTION 15–20 foot (4.5–6 m) tall tree

HARDY ZONES 9–11

PLANT Plant sapling in spring or fall.

SPACE 12–25 feet (3.5–7.5 m)

CARE Water moderately. Side dress every 4–6 weeks.

HARVEST Harvest when the fruit is pink or yellow.

DISEASES/PESTS Address pests such as red spider mites, thrips, scale, and mealybugs with insect oil or soap. Remove and destroy caterpillars by hand.

VARIETIES/CULTIVARS Ruby Red, pink, white

POINT OF FACT The grapefruit's name alludes to the fruit clusters on the tree, which look like giant grape clusters. Ruby Red was the first grapefruit patent.

○ I GREW IT!

WHEN I GREW IT
DATE

NOTES

TREE
Guava
(Psidium guajava)

DESCRIPTION 20-foot (6 m) tall fruit tree

HARDY ZONES 9–12

PLANT Plant sapling in the spring.

SPACE 16 feet (5 m)

CARE Water moderately. Side dress every 1–3 months while young and then 3 to 4 times per year as the tree matures.

HARVEST Harvest fruit 90–150 days after the flowers bloom, when it is tender and ripe.

DISEASES/PESTS Choose anthracnose-resistant varieties.

VARIETIES/CULTIVARS Ruby supreme

POINT OF FACT A guava contains 4 times more vitamin C than an orange. Guava is native to Mexico, Central America, South America, and the Caribbean region.

I GREW IT!

WHEN I GREW IT
DATE

NOTES

Huckleberry

(Vaccinium ovatum)

DESCRIPTION 2–10 foot (0.5–3 m) tall fruit shrub

HARDY ZONES 2–9

PLANT Plant young shrubs in acidic soil. Note that huckleberry plants do best in the wild. Blueberries are a better fit for the garden.

NOTE: Grows taller in the shade

SPACE 3–4 feet (91–122 cm)

CARE Water moderately.

HARVEST Harvest from mid-August through mid-September.

DISEASES/PESTS Deter birds with netting.

POINT OF FACT Nearly all huckleberries grow in the wild, mostly in national parks. They look like blueberries but have 10 little seeds inside, giving them a crunch.

I GREW IT!

WHEN I GREW IT
DATE

NOTES

VINE

Kiwi

(Actinidia deliciosa—subtropical; Actinidia arguta and Actinidia kolomikta—hardy)

DESCRIPTION 40-foot (12 m) fruit vine

HARDY ZONES 3–9, depending on species

PLANT Plant young vines beside supports on which the vines can grow.

SPACE 10 feet (3 m)

CARE Water moderately. Side dress twice a year.

HARVEST Harvest the fruit in late August to early September, usually in the second or third growing season. Carefully pull the fragile fruit from the vine.

DISEASES/PESTS Avoid disease with good soil drainage.

POINT OF FACT The hardy kiwi is thinner skinned and eaten like grapes. However, the thick brown skin of subtropical kiwis is also edible.

I GREW IT!

WHEN I GREW IT
DATE

NOTES

SHRUB
Kumquat
(Citrus japonica)

DESCRIPTION 8–15 foot (2–4.5 m) tall fruit shrub

HARDY ZONES 9–10

PLANT Plant sapling in the spring.

SPACE 8 feet (2 m)

CARE Water moderately. Side dress each spring.

HARVEST Harvest fruit when the skin is deep orange and tender.

DISEASES/PESTS Address pests such as red spider mites, thrips, scale, and mealybugs with insect oil or soap. Remove and destroy caterpillars by hand.

VARIETIES/CULTIVARS nagami, nordmann

POINT OF FACT Kumquats have a sweet rind and sour flesh, opposite from other citrus fruits. The kumquat plant is native to South Asia and the Asia-Pacific region.

I GREW IT!

WHEN I GREW IT
DATE

NOTES

....

TREE

Lemon
(Citrus limon)

DESCRIPTION 10–20 foot (3–6 m) tall fruit tree

HARDY ZONES 9–11, or in a container to be moved indoors

PLANT Plant sapling in the ground or in a container in spring.

SPACE 10–25 feet (3–7.5 m)

CARE Water moderately.

HARVEST Harvest lemons when they turn fully yellow. Harvest time varies by type.

DISEASES/PESTS Address pests such as red spider mites, thrips, scale, and mealybugs with insect oil or soap. Remove and destroy caterpillars by hand.

VARIETIES/CULTIVARS Eureka, Harvey, Meyer

POINT OF FACT Lemon tree leaves are used in cooking and then removed, like a bay leaf. Lemons are native to Asia.

 **I GREW IT!**

WHEN I GREW IT
DATE

NOTES

TREE
Lime
(Citrus × latifolia and *C. × aurantifolia)*

DESCRIPTION Citrus hybrid trees, with thorns, growing 10–16 feet (3–5 m) tall and producing fruit best eaten when unripe

HARDY ZONES 9–11

PLANT Plant a sapling in the ground. You can try to start with a seed, but it takes trial and error.

SPACE 10–25 feet (3–7.5 m)

CARE Water moderately. Side dress every 2 months.

HARVEST Harvest limes while they are still green. They turn yellow when mature but taste better while immature.

DISEASES/PESTS Address pests such as red spider mites, thrips, scale, and mealybugs with insect oil or soap. Remove and destroy caterpillars by hand.

POINT OF FACT To prevent scurvy during the 19th century, British sailors were issued a daily allowance of citrus, such as lemon or lime. The acid in lime juice "cooks" fish without heating it. It's how the dish ceviche is made.

I GREW IT!

WHEN I GREW IT
DATE

NOTES

TREE
Mango Tree
(Mangifera indica)

DESCRIPTION 6.5–100 foot (2–30 m) tall fruit tree

HARDY ZONES 10–11 (Even in a container, they are best grown outdoors.)

PLANT Plant sapling in a large pot in the spring.

SPACE 13 feet (4 m)

CARE Water heavily. Side dress once a month during spring and summer.

HARVEST Harvest fruit when they are tender.

DISEASES/PESTS Avoid anthracnose and powdery mildew by ensuring proper drainage.

VARIETIES/CULTIVARS okrong, nuan chan, yaigrum

POINT OF FACT Mangos are native to India. Most of an orangutan's diet is fruit, including mangos.

I GREW IT!

WHEN I GREW IT
DATE

NOTES

Olive Tree
(Olea europaea)

DESCRIPTION 25–50 foot (7.5–15 m) tall tree with thorny branches

HARDY ZONES 8–11, or in a container to be moved indoors

PLANT Plant a sapling in a container in cactus potting mix or in the ground.

SPACE 10 feet (3 m)

CARE Water moderately. For container plants, pot up each year, and move the plant outside after the last frost. Fertilize monthly while it is blooming and producing fruit.

HARVEST Harvest August–November. Unripe green olives must be brined; ripe black olives can be eaten raw.

DISEASES/PESTS Set traps for olive fruit flies.

VARIETIES/CULTIVARS chemlali, pendolino, picual

POINT OF FACT The wild olive tree was domesticated 6,000–8,000 years ago in the Middle East. The olive branch symbolizes peace.

I GREW IT!

WHEN I GREW IT
DATE

NOTES

TREE

Orange Tree
(Citrus x sinensis)

DESCRIPTION Citrus hybrids growing 8–25 feet (2–7.5 m) and producing orange fruit

HARDY ZONES 8–11

PLANT Plant a sapling in spring.

SPACE 10–25 feet (3–7.5 m)

CARE Water moderately; fertilize monthly.

HARVEST Harvest when fully ripe.

DISEASES/PESTS Address pests such as red spider mites, thrips, scale, and mealybugs with insect oil or soap. Remove and destroy caterpillars by hand.

VARIETIES/CULTIVARS Valencia, Washington naval, sanguinelli

POINT OF FACT There are over 600 varieties of orange trees. Florida produces more than 70 percent of US citrus, with most of it processed into juice.

WHEN I GREW IT
DATE

NOTES

TREE

Papaya
(Carica papaya)

DESCRIPTION 15–30 foot (4.5–10 m) tall fruit tree

HARDY ZONES 9–11

PLANT Plant saplings in the ground.

SPACE 8–10 feet (2–3 m)

CARE Water moderately, and fertilize monthly.

HARVEST Harvest when the fruit is tender and ripe.

DISEASES/PESTS Avoid common diseases with proper drainage.

VARIETIES/CULTIVARS sunset, sunrise, kapoho solo

POINT OF FACT The stems and bark of papaya are used in the production of ropes. Papayas are native to southern Mexico and Central America, but now grow in many tropical regions.

WHEN I GREW IT
DATE

NOTES

....

PERENNIAL

Passion fruit

(Passiflora edulis and *P. edulis flavicarpa)*

DESCRIPTION 30–40 foot (9–12 m) vine producing large fruit

HARDY ZONES 9–11

PLANT Plant young vines in the spring, beside scaffolding for the vine.

SPACE 4 feet (1 m)

CARE Water heavily, and fertilize twice a year.

HARVEST Harvest fruits in summer, usually a year and a half after planting.

DISEASES/PESTS Prevent common diseases by ensuring proper drainage.

VARIETIES/CULTIVARS Australian purple, common purple, yee selection

POINT OF FACT In Sri Lanka, passion fruit juice is one of the most popular refreshments. Passion fruit is often added to other juices to enhance their aroma.

I GREW IT!

WHEN I GREW IT

DATE

NOTES

Pawpaw

(Asimina triloba)

to

DESCRIPTION 20-foot (6 m) tall fruit tree

HARDY ZONES 5–9

PLANT Plant a sapling in the ground in the spring. Pawpaws need filtered sunlight the first 2 years but require full sun to fruit.

SPACE 10 feet (3 m)

CARE Water moderately. Fertilize monthly March–June.

HARVEST Harvest fruit mid-August through September, when fruit is soft to the touch.

DISEASES/PESTS Trap slugs and snails with potato bait.

VARIETIES/CULTIVARS sunflower, taylor, taytwo

POINT OF FACT The pawpaw is the largest edible fruit native to the United States. Though it grows in cooler climates, the pawpaw tree has a tropical appearance, and the fruit's flavor is a combination of mango, banana, and citrus.

 **I GREW IT!**

WHEN I GREW IT
DATE

NOTES

....

Peach Tree
(Prunus persica)

DESCRIPTION A fruit tree that is 8–10 feet (2–3 m) tall for dwarf varieties and 12–15 feet (3.5–4.5 m) tall for full-size varieties

HARDY ZONES 5–8

PLANT Plant a sapling in the ground or in a container in spring or fall.

SPACE 12–15 feet (3.5–4.5 meters)

CARE Water moderately. Side dress in the spring once the tree is 2 years old.

HARVEST Harvest July–September when the fruit is tender and ripe.

DISEASES/PESTS Control pests with orchard spray.

VARIETIES/CULTIVARS bounty, Arctic jay, Rich May

POINT OF FACT Peaches are categorized as freestone (the stone easily pops out), clingstone (the stone clings to the peach), and semi-freestone. Nectarines are peaches with a recessive trait of having no fuzz.

◖ **I GREW IT!** ▷

WHEN I GREW IT
DATE

NOTES

Peanut
(Arachis hypogaea)

DESCRIPTION 12–20 inch (30.5–51 cm) tall plant that produces pods known as peanuts
NOTE: Some people are allergic to peanuts.

HARDY ZONES 5–10

PLANT Plant seedlings in the soil. Seeds (uncooked peanuts still in their shells) can be started inside by filling a container with potting mix, shelling the peanuts, and covering them with an inch of soil. They will soon sprout.

SPACE 6–8 inches (15–20.5 cm)

CARE Water moderately.

HARVEST Harvest in fall when the leaves begin to yellow. The pods mature underground. Pull up the whole plant to harvest them.

DISEASES/PESTS Avoid diseases and pests by ensuring proper drainage.

VARIETIES/CULTIVARS Carwile's Virginia, Early Spanish, Tennessee red Valencia

POINT OF FACT It takes about 540 peanuts to make a 12-ounce jar of peanut butter. Peanuts are not nuts. They are legumes related to peas and beans.

◖ I GREW IT! ▷

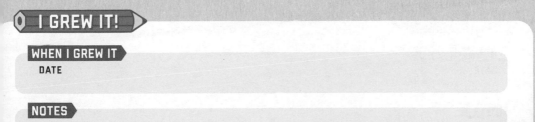

WHEN I GREW IT
DATE

NOTES

....

Pecan Tree
(Carya illinoinensis)

DESCRIPTION 70–100 foot (21–30 m) tall nut tree

HARDY ZONES 5–9

PLANT Plant a sapling in spring or fall.

SPACE 40–70 feet (12–21 m)

CARE Water moderately.

HARVEST Harvest pecans September–November as soon as they drop.

DISEASES/PESTS Control pests with insect soap; rake out webworm webs.

VARIETIES/CULTIVARS Stuart, desirable, Cape Fear

POINT OF FACT Native to North America, "pecan" derives its name from an Algonquin word meaning any nut requiring a stone to crack. Pecan pie is an American creation.

◦ I GREW IT!

WHEN I GREW IT
DATE

NOTES

Pine nut
(Pinus)

DESCRIPTION A genus of trees 50–150 foot (15–45.5 m) tall, some of which produce pine nuts large enough to gather and eat

HARDY ZONES 1–10, depending on the species

PLANT Plant saplings in the ground in the spring or fall. (NOTE: They take 15–25 years to produce pine nuts and even longer to reach full production. Most US-gathered pine nuts come from wild trees.)

SPACE 10–12 feet (3–3.5 m)

CARE Water moderately. Fertilize yearly.

HARVEST Harvest pine nuts before the green cone begins to open. Dry the cones in the sun in a bag for 20 days. Smash the cones and separate the seeds by hand.

DISEASES/PESTS Pines can defend themselves against insects as long as they are kept strong with fertilizer and water during droughts.

VARIETIES/CULTIVARS Mexican pinon, Colorado pinon

POINT OF FACT For some people, pine nuts can make everything taste metallic for several weeks.

◖ I GREW IT! ▷

WHEN I GREW IT
   DATE

NOTES

....

Pineapple

(Ananas comosus)

DESCRIPTION 3–6 foot (1–2 m) tall and wide fruit plant

HARDY ZONES 11–12, or in a container

PLANT Plant the top of a pineapple. Twist it off the fruit, pull off about 5 leaves from the bottom, and then allow it to dry for 1 week. Plant it in a container with cactus potting mix. Place outside in the sun but move indoors to a sunny window before the first frost.

SPACE 3–5 feet (1–1.5 m)

CARE Water lightly.

HARVEST Harvest a pineapple in about 2 years. When it is ripe, cut it from the plant with a sharp kitchen knife where the pineapple joins the stalk. It will take another 2 years before the next pineapple grows! If you'd like, plant the pineapple top for a second plant.

DISEASES/PESTS Pick off mealybugs or deter them with insect soap or horticultural oil.

VARIETIES/CULTIVARS Smooth cayenne, natal queen, red Spanish

POINT OF FACT Hawaii produces about one third of all pineapples in the world. Pineapples ripen faster upside down.

I GREW IT!

WHEN I GREW IT

DATE

NOTES

Pistachio Tree
(Pistacia vera)

DESCRIPTION 25–30 foot (7.5–9 m) tall nut tree

HARDY ZONES 8–10

PLANT In the fall, plant 2 saplings, a male and a female, for cross-pollination.

SPACE 20 feet (6 m)

CARE Water heavily.

HARVEST Harvest nuts after 5–8 years. Hit the branches with a heavy pole to dislodge the nuts.

DISEASES/PESTS Fungal infections occur in poor environments. Pistachios need long, hot summers and cold winters.

VARIETIES/CULTIVARS Joley, red aleppo, lassen

POINT OF FACT The pistachio shell opens itself as the kernel grows. In China, pistachios are known as the "happy nut" because they look like they're smiling.

WHEN I GREW IT
DATE

NOTES

....

285

Plum Tree
(Prunus subgenus Prunus)

DESCRIPTION 10–25 foot (3–8 m) tall fruit tree

HARDY ZONES 3–8

PLANT Plant saplings in early spring.

SPACE 20–25 feet (6–7.5 m) for standard trees and 10–15 feet (3–4.5 m) for dwarf trees

CARE Water moderately.

HARVEST After 4–6 years, harvest in summer and fall when the fruit is tender.

DISEASES/PESTS Prune overcrowded branches to avoid disease.

VARIETIES/CULTIVARS Damson, greengage, Mirabelle

POINT OF FACT Plums may have been one of the first fruits domesticated by humans. Honeybees are the main pollinators of plum trees.

◖ **I GREW IT!** ▷

WHEN I GREW IT
DATE

NOTES

TREE

Pomegranate
(Punica granatum)

DESCRIPTION 12–16 foot (3.5–5 m) tall shrub or tree

HARDY ZONES 7–11

PLANT Plant saplings in late winter or early spring.

SPACE 10 feet (3 m)

CARE Water moderately.

HARVEST Harvest after 2–3 years. Ripe fruit makes a metallic sound when you tap it with your finger.

DISEASES/PESTS Remove old fruit and dead branches to reduce fungal infection.

VARIETIES/CULTIVARS Ambrosia, ariana, eversweet

POINT OF FACT Pomegranate trees can live for over 200 years.

I GREW IT!

WHEN I GREW IT
DATE

NOTES

Raspberries

(Rubus idaeus)

DESCRIPTION 6-foot (2 m) tall cane plant

HARDY ZONES 4–8

PLANT Plant young plants in early spring.

SPACE Red and yellow: 3 feet (1 m); purple and black: 4 feet (1.5 m)

CARE Water moderately. Prune dead canes each year.

HARVEST Harvest raspberries from midsummer to fall starting the first year. Check for ripe raspberries every 2 or 3 days.

DISEASES/PESTS Combat fruit worm with horticultural oil or insect soap.

VARIETIES/CULTIVARS Amity, Autumn bliss, boyne

POINT OF FACT Raspberries are related to blackberries and roses.

I GREW IT!

WHEN I GREW IT

DATE

NOTES

SHRUB

Red and White Currants

(Ribes rubrum)

DESCRIPTION 3-foot (91 cm) tall fruit bush

HARDY ZONES 3–8

PLANT Plant young shrubs in fall or winter.

SPACE 5 feet (1.5 m)

CARE Water moderately.

HARVEST Harvest 2 years after planting. Taste berries—they are ready when sweet and tart.

DISEASES/PESTS Remove diseased branches.

VARIETIES/CULTIVARS Red lake, white Dutch

POINT OF FACT White currants are translucent and have a sweeter taste than red currants. Like raisins, currants are popular in baking.

 **I GREW IT!**

WHEN I GREW IT
DATE

NOTES

Serviceberry (Juneberry)

(Amelanchier arborea)

to

DESCRIPTION 20–50 foot (6–15 m) tree

HARDY ZONES 4–8

PLANT Plant saplings in the spring.

SPACE 12–15 feet (4–5 m)

CARE Water moderately to heavily.

HARVEST Harvest fruit 2–3 years after planting. In June or July, pick bunches by hand when they are purplish blue or purplish red. Then remove the berries from the stems.

DISEASES/PESTS Serviceberry rust can be controlled with fungicide.

POINT OF FACT It is also called a juneberry because it typically ripens in June. Serviceberries taste like blueberries and can be eaten raw or baked in desserts.

I GREW IT!

WHEN I GREW IT
DATE

NOTES

Strawberries

(Fragaria x ananassa)

DESCRIPTION Low-growing plant that produces fruit

HARDY ZONES 3–10

PLANT Plant seedlings in early spring.

SPACE 24 inches (61 cm)

CARE Water heavily. Surround plants with straw.

HARVEST Harvest strawberries in the second year, when they turn red.

DISEASES/PESTS Wash the plants once a week with soapy water or neem oil. This will keep bugs off.

VARIETIES/CULTIVARS Honeoye, allstar, Ozark beauty

POINT OF FACT Strawberries are among the first fruits to ripen each spring. There are 200 seeds on an average strawberry.

I GREW IT!

WHEN I GREW IT
DATE

NOTES

ANNUAL

Watermelon

(Citrullus lanatus)

DESCRIPTION A vine that produces large fruit

HARDY ZONES 3–11

PLANT Plant seeds on a mound after the last frost.

SPACE 18–24 inches (45.5–61 cm) between mounds

CARE Water heavily. Prune the vine to achieve high-quality fruit. Pinch off the vine after 5 leaves form. Allow just 1 fruit to grow per 5-leaf vine section. Pinch off others.

HARVEST Harvest when fruit is tender and aromatic.

DISEASES/PESTS Avoid powdery mildew by ensuring proper sunlight, drainage, and spacing.

VARIETIES/CULTIVARS crimson sweet, golden midget, little baby flower

POINT OF FACT Watermelon is native to the Kalahari Desert in Africa. It is not actually harmful to eat a watermelon seed. The whole fruit is edible.

○ I GREW IT!

WHEN I GREW IT
DATE

NOTES

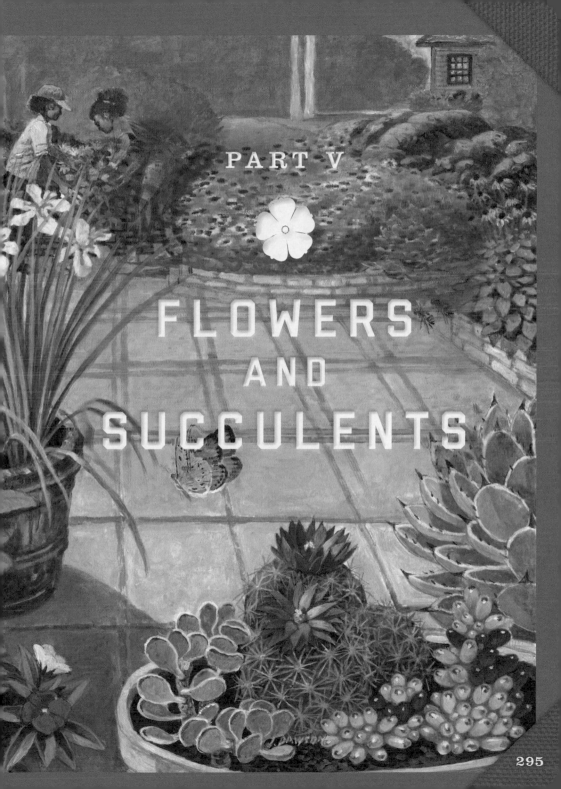

PART V

FLOWERS
AND
SUCCULENTS

What would YOU do?

When you think of a garden, one word

comes to mind: food. Then Nana comes to visit. She pulls down a vase and hands you a pair of scissors. "Bring me some flowers from the garden, please," she says. Flowers? You're growing herbs and vegetables and even a cherry tree, but what is the point of growing something you can't eat? "Nana, I grow food, not flowers," you explain. She laughs and says, "But flowers are food for the soul. You must plant flowers." *What would you do?*

CHAPTER 1

Annuals

Most plants have flowers, but here we refer to the beauty queens of the flower world (sorry, broccoli). Flowers grow on stems, bushes, or trees. Bushes and trees are always perennials. Stem, or nonwoody, flowers can be either annuals, biennials, or perennials. Whether food or flower, annuals last just one year, biennials two years, and perennials more than that. Annuals are often the first plants grown by new gardeners, who return to them each season for their color and cheer. Often, they are grown in flower boxes or pots, whereas biennials and perennials reside in a permanent plot. In a container environment, annuals need rich potting mix and ample water. You can also deadhead the flowers to encourage new buds.

ZINNIA

DOGWOOD

MORNING GLORY

WHAT YOU'LL NEED

➢ flowers growing in your garden, scissors (optional)

Many annuals will produce flowers throughout the season. You can encourage this by deadheading wilted flowers. This way, the plant will stop sending food and water to the dead flower and instead funnel that energy toward new growth. To do this, cut or pinch off the dead flower just above the next set of leaves.

I DID IT! DATE:

COSMOS

SIBERIAN LARKSPUR

MARIGOLD

Annuals are often planted as seedlings for an immediate pop of color in the spring. However, plants such as zinnias and cosmos sprout so quickly that you can save money by planting seeds. Even giant sunflowers can be grown quickly from seed. At the end of the season, most annuals will be discarded. However, some will self-seed if you leave their dead flowers intact. Others can be brought indoors as houseplants. These are not true annuals, but perennials that cannot survive the cold winters in most of the country. In the southernmost regions, they can be left in the ground year-round.

Annuals That Are Not Really Annuals

Grow these as perennials if you have mild winters, or move them indoors before the first frost:

POINSETTIA   IMPATIENS   GERANIUM

> **WHAT YOU'LL NEED**
>
> ➢ a large pot, potting mix, three types of annual flowers, a trowel or spoon

A popular expression when planting a flowerpot is to choose "a thriller, a filler, and a spiller." The thriller is a tall, splashy plant, the filler is any plant that provides full foliage, and the spiller is a vining plant that will "spill" over the edge.

THRILLER sunflower, cosmos, geranium

FILLER impatiens, pansy, petunia

SPILLER trailing petunia, sweet potato vine, nasturtium

Plant the thriller in either the center or back center of the pot. The potting mix should just cover the soil surrounding the plants' roots. Plant the filler in front of or around the thriller. Plant the spiller around the front edge or all around the pot.

I DID IT! DATE:

Sunflower Varieties

AMERICAN GIANT

Growing 15 feet (4.5 m) tall with giant flowers, this sunflower brings the drama.

AMERICAN GIANT

EARTH WALKER

This tall sunflower blooms in a range of "earthy" colors, from red to orange.

EARTH WALKER

DWARF

Large flowers but short stalks make it an ideal sunflower for pots.

DWARF

SUNNY SMILE

Another shorter stalked variety, this sunflower has a unique flower that almost looks like an emoji.

SUNNY SMILE

TEDDY BEAR

As its name suggests, this shorter variety has a fuzzy, fluffy flower.

TEDDY BEAR

CHAPTER 2

Perennials

Perennials are any plant that lives three or more years. (Biennials last two years.) They are typically grown in a flower bed, though they can be grown year after year in containers. Perennials bloom for a shorter period than annuals, so gardeners often plant varieties that bloom at different points in the growing season. Once your perennials are planted, you can deadhead them to force more blooms, or allow them to bloom, wilt, and go into winter dormancy. Early in the spring, cut back dead plants so that new stems can sprout. The plants should be side dressed to replace the nutrients consumed by the flowers the year before. Perennials have a tendency to spread. When they become crowded, divide them in early spring by digging them up and pulling them apart at the roots, and then replanting half in another container or hole. This usually only needs to be done once every three years. Depending on the plant, perennials are planted as seeds, seedlings, or bulbs. Seedlings can have root balls or bare roots.

SEEDLING
(DAISY)

BARE ROOT SEEDLING
(PEONY)

BULBS
(TULIP)

Attract Bees, Birds, and Butterflies to Your Garden

Bees, birds, and butterflies pollinate plants and are fun to watch. You can attract them to your garden in many ways.

Start a compost heap. Besides keeping food waste out of landfills and building nutrient-rich soil, compost heaps are a feast for birds, bees, and butterflies.

Bees go buzzy over purple and blue flowers, which tend to have the most abundant nectar among flowers. Try aster, bee balm, cosmos, foxgloves, lilac, phlox, and many herbs with purple blossoms.

Plant foods caterpillars like. For instance, monarchs eat milkweed, and swallowtails prefer herbs such as fennel, dill, and parsley.

Provide water. Place a large bowl of water in the shade. Add a few simple water plants, which will keep the water clean and provide resting spots for butterflies. Change the water every two weeks to avoid algae growth and mosquito breeding.

Provide shelter. Shrubs and trees are nesting grounds for birds, and pollen providers to butterflies and bees.

Make peace with nature. Wild plants can be a pain for the very reason they succeed in nature: They pop up everywhere and outcompete other plants in the garden. However, birds, butterflies, and bees love native plants such as trumpet vine and grapevine. Rather than eradicating them, simply cut them back each year to keep them under control.

TAKE IT TO THE **NEXT LEVEL** ↗

Plant a Fairy Garden

Why not plant a restful place for the fairies, too?

> **WHAT YOU'LL NEED** ›
>
> ➤ a wide pot; trowel or spoon; potting mix; Irish or Scottish moss; a fairy "tree": rosemary bush; a fairy "shrub": sea pinks; milk carton; bark and sticks; hot glue gun; wire; and pebbles for a path

STEP 1 › Make the fairy house. Using the hot glue gun, apply sticks and bark to the milk carton to build the house.

STEP 2 › Make 2 small holes at the bottom of the house. Thread the wire through the holes so that several inches of wire trail down from the house.

STEP 3 › Prune the rosemary bush in the shape of a fir tree.

STEP 4 › Fill the pot with potting mix.

STEP 5 › Plant the fairy "tree," burying the roots.

STEP 6 › Plant the fairy "shrub," burying the roots.

STEP 7 › Plant the moss, burying the roots.

STEP 8 › Attach the house by pressing the ends of the wires into the moss and deep into the potting mix.

STEP 9 › Water the plants by spraying generously once a week.

I DID IT! DATE:

CHAPTER 3

Floral Trees and Shrubs

Planting trees and shrubs will likely be a family decision, because they take up space and live for several years. Things to consider are: What will they add to your outdoor space? Floral trees and shrubs beautify homes, provide privacy, and attract birds and butterflies. How large will they grow? Tree size varies widely. Where should you plant it? Top choices are the front yard or along the perimeter of the yard. Here, they soften the edges and provide privacy and shade. You don't want to plant them too close to a home, lest they damage the foundation as they grow. Next, what shade will they provide? Shade is a welcome addition to most outdoor spaces. However, you don't want to create so much shade that there is nowhere for full-sun plants to grow. Measure the space the canopy will fill at maturity to determine how much of the yard will be shaded.

Finally, what care will they need? Bushes and shrubs generally require watering and fertilizing at the start of their lives, but little care as they mature.

WATER OAK

Bush or Shrub?

What's the difference between a bush and shrub? Both are woody, like trees, but lower to the ground. Some consider a bush to be wild and a shrub to be planted. Others think of bushes as being low to the ground whereas shrubs are akin to small trees. And some simply use them as synonyms. Whatever you call them, these floral perennials will add scent and beauty to your garden for years.

Cut Flower Bushes and Shrubs

Big flowers mean big impact. Their scent wafts across the neighborhood and can be enjoyed indoors, too. For cutting flowers, try planting a lilac, snowball, gardenia, camelia, or peony bush. Be sure to allow for enough space as the bush matures!

Hydrangea Color and pH

The color of hydrangea blooms depends on the pH of the soil. Blue hydrangeas grow in acidic soil (5.5 pH or less). Purple hydrangeas grow in near-neutral soil (5.5–6.5 pH). Pink hydrangeas grow in alkaline soil (6.5 pH or higher).

Grow a Lilac Bush for Free

WHAT YOU'LL NEED

➤ the sucker from a lilac bush growing in a friend's garden, a shovel, prepared garden soil

STEP 1 Begin in spring or fall. Ask someone who has a lilac bush if you can collect one of the *suckers*. They are the green shoots growing at the woody base of the plant.

STEP 2 Dig up the sucker, keeping its roots intact.

STEP 3 Back home, prepare a 12-inch (30.5 cm) diameter circle of soil so that it is loose and nutrient-rich. If your soil is poor, dig a 12-inch (30.5 cm) hole and replace it with garden soil and mulch.

STEP 4 In the prepared area, dig a hole 6 inches (15 cm) deep. Place the sucker in the hole. If the roots are bare, make a small mound inside the hole and spread them over it. Fill the hole with the garden soil. Add mulch around the base. If you are planting more than one bush, allow 5–15 feet (1.5–4.5 m) in between.

STEP 5 Water moderately throughout the spring and summer. In 3–4 years, you will have a big, blooming lilac bush.

I DID IT! DATE:

Roses

Roses hold a special place among the flowers. There are rose societies, rose shows, rose parades, and rose balls. Roses mean love. And many gardeners consider roses to be their claim to fame. Roses fall into three categories. Species roses include wild roses and their closest relatives. The flowers are smaller and simpler than the newer varieties, but they are best at producing rose hips, which can be brewed into tea. Old garden roses date to ancient times. The full bushes with fluffy flowers are what you might picture growing around an English cottage. Finally, modern roses, first cultivated in 1867, are the long-stemmed varieties given on Valentine's Day. The most popular roses in the world, hybrid tea roses, fall into this category.

WRINKLED ROSE

CLIMBING ROSE

ROSE HIPS

ROSE

Grow a Rose Bush

WHAT YOU'LL NEED

➤ a full-sun location with garden soil that is loose and nutrient-rich, a bare root or potted rose bush, a shovel, garden snips, and fertilizer

STEP 1 If you order a bare root plant, keep it in a cool dry place until you're ready to plant. Then, 12 hours before planting, soak the roots in water.

STEP 2 Two weeks after the first frost, dig an 18-inch (45.5 cm) wide, 12-inch (30.5 cm) deep hole.

12 INCHES (30.5 CM) DEEP

18 INCHES (45.5 CM)
WIDE

STEP 3 For bare root plants, create a 10-inch (25 cm) high mound inside the hole. Spread the roots out over the mound. For potted plants, simply set the soil ball in the hole.

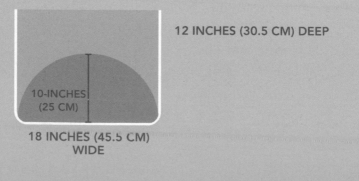

12 INCHES (30.5 CM) DEEP

10-INCHES
(25 CM)

18 INCHES (45.5 CM)
WIDE

STEP 4 Fill the hole with a combination of garden soil and mulch.

STEP 5 Water deeply.

STEP 6 Continue to water deeply once or twice a week, depending on how warm it is.

STEP 7 When flowers bloom and die, "deadhead" them by snipping the branch 3 leaves down.

STEP 8 Four weeks before the first frost, stop deadheading to discourage new growth that could be damaged by the frost.

STEP 9 Allow the bush to go dormant.

STEP 10 In the spring, prune the bush, removing dead flowers and branches.

I DID IT! DATE:

Climbers

Climbing perennials add living color to fences, walls, and archways. In grow zones 9–12, try bougainvillea, a thick pink bush that grows up houses and stone walls. It should be pruned before it reaches gutters and roofs, lest it cause damage. In cooler grow zones, wisteria is a beautiful choice. However, it is aggressive and should not be planted near a home. In the yard, it should be trimmed back yearly so that it doesn't take over. Another good choice is clematis. The vine begins daintily, but thickens in time, so provide a thin but sturdy structure on which it can grow.

BUTTONBUSH

Native Shrubs

Native plants have evolved to survive whatever nature throws at them, whether that's heat, cold, drought, or swampiness. They also provide the best habitats for native animals. Buttonbush is a tall, spreading bush that attracts pollinators (grow zones 5–9). Its flowers and fruit look like buttons. Low on space? Plant the New Jersey tea bush (grow zones 4–8). It's popular with pollinators, and people have historically dried the leaves for tea.

Floral Trees

Floral trees are the magic wands of the plant world. They fill the air with perfume, attract the prettiest birds, and carpet the ground with petals. When you plant a floral tree, you add to the magic. But do you have the space, budget, and time? Floral trees can grow to towering heights. Though slow growing, the magnolia eventually stretches up to 80 feet (24 m) tall. However, a standard redbud grows to just 20 feet (6 m), and the weeping redbud, to 6 feet (2 m). Dwarf varieties are available for most floral species.

Trees are more expensive than smaller garden plants. Save money by purchasing trees on sale in the fall. In terms of time commitment, a tree must be planted, watered, and trimmed. Cut down on time by planting a native floral, which will be hardier and need less watering. Luckily, some of the most popular florals are native to North America. They include magnolias, redbuds, dogwoods, and hawthorns.

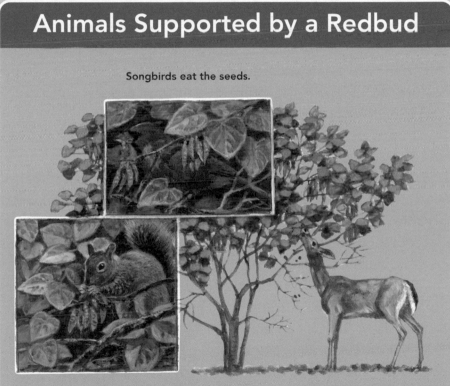

Animals Supported by a Redbud

Songbirds eat the seeds.

Squirrels eat the bud, bark, and seeds.

Whitetail deer eat twigs and leaves.

CHAPTER 4

Succulents

In arid and semiarid climates, succulents are the ornamental plants of choice. Because the air inside homes is also dry, succulents make good houseplants. A succulent is a plant that has adapted to dry climates by storing water in its thick flesh. Among the succulents, cacti have thick stems and thin, spiky leaves, whereas other succulents have thick stems and leaves. Succulents can be tiny or tall, but they are always low maintenance due to their adaptation to tough desert conditions.

An Outdoor Succulent Garden

Succulents thrive in areas with less than 25 inches (63.5 cm) of rain per year. If you draw a slightly curved line midway through Minnesota and down to the tip of Texas, the land to the west is arid or semiarid until you reach coastal Northern California, Oregon, and Washington.

Most succulents prefer the climate of zones 9–11, found in Texas, New Mexico, Arizona, Nevada, Utah, and California.

In these zones, plant succulents in the ground in the spring. Unlike with most plants, refrain from watering during the first week. Then give them a good soaking. Unless your

ZONE 1 ■ ZONE 4 ■ ZONE 7 ■ ZONE 10 ■
ZONE 2 ■ ZONE 5 ■ ZONE 8 ■ ZONE 11 ■
ZONE 3 ■ ZONE 6 ■ ZONE 9 ■

weather is very hot, succulents in the ground can go without water or fertilizer. In the hot valleys of the Southwest, they may need some of both. In this area, fertilize in the spring and winter with a cactus mix or fish emulsion. Water twice a week during the hot months. Also, note that though succulents are heat lovers, they prefer some shade when temperatures rise above 90 degrees. Succulents don't need pruning, other than removal of dead parts. If you choose to prune a succulent for a desired size or shape, do this in the winter. And take care: Some succulents contain sap that burns the skin and eyes.

TRACK IT ↘ Measure Rainfall

Meteorologists use an 8-inch (20.5 cm) diameter cylinder called a rain gauge to measure rainfall. You can purchase one at a garden store or online. Placement is important. It should be as far away from tall structures, such as your house and trees, as possible to avoid runoff or blockage. The opening should be above any grass or foliage.

Record the date of rainfall and the amount of rain that fell.

Date:	Amount of rain:

Grow a Cactus

WHAT YOU'LL NEED

➢ prepared garden soil or a pot filled with cactus soil, shovel or trowel, cut-resistant gloves

If you live in a warm, arid, or semiarid climate, you can plant a cactus in the ground. In cool but still dry climates, you can plant a cold-hardy succulent (see sidebar page 318) in the ground. Otherwise, plant your cactus in a pot to be moved indoors in cold or wet seasons. Note that you will need to use cactus gloves or other cut-resistant gloves to avoid being poked by the spines.

STEP 1 ▸ Dig a hole large enough to fit the cactus's root ball.

STEP 2 ▸ Place the cactus in the ground (or in a large pot, with equal parts cactus soil and potting soil).

STEP 3 ▸ Water moderately for the first 4 weeks. Then the cactus will receive the moisture it needs from the soil. (Pots dry out faster than the ground. A cactus in a pot needs to be watered—or rained on—once monthly in winter and every week or every other week in summer.)

I DID IT! DATE:

316

Grow a Cactus Garden

STEP 1 Once you have 1 cactus, you can grow another beside it, allowing at least 1 foot (30.5 cm) between small cacti, and 3 feet (91 cm) between large ones. You may want to space them farther apart, however, in keeping with the natural look of a sparse desert landscape.

STEP 2 Save money by propagating your existing cacti or swapping cuttings with a neighbor.

STEP 3 For a cutting, cut with snips a piece at least 4 inches (10 cm) long. Allow it to dry out for several days, until the cut part is dry. Then plant the cutting in a pot, cut side down. Allow roots to grow for several months, watering lightly. Then transplant it into the ground.

I DID IT! DATE:

Five Cold-Hardy Succulents

Some succulents grow in dry but cooler climates. Before planting, check for the minimum temperature succulents can endure.

DELOSPERMA COOPERI

OPUNTIA FICUS-INDICA

ESCOBARIA VIVIPARA

SEDUM RUBROTINCTUM

AGAVE PARRYI

Succulents in Containers

Where summer is hot and winter is cold, succulents can be grown as indoor-outdoor plants. They will tolerate heavy summer storms because soaring temperatures afterward dry them out. Succulents in containers should be watered only when the soil is dry two inches deep. This usually means weekly water in spring and summer and monthly watering during the winter.

Make a Succulent Terrarium

WHAT YOU'LL NEED

➢ a large mason jar, pebbles, cactus mix and potting mix, a succulent cutting or plant, and a trowel or spoon

STEP 1 Fill the jar 1 inch (2.5 cm) deep with pebbles.

STEP 2 Add 2 inches (5 cm) of potting mix and cactus mix in equal parts.

STEP 3 Plant the cutting or plant.

STEP 4 Add pebbles on the top and any decorations of your choosing (plastic dinosaurs, a fairy, etc.).

STEP 5 Do not water for a week. Then water weekly in spring and summer, or every 2 weeks in fall and winter.

I DID IT! DATE:

FLOWER GUIDE

Flowers brighten up every garden. Choose between annual or perennial—or a mix of both—to keep your garden blooming throughout the warmer months.

LIGHT NEEDS

Full sun

Partial sun

Partial shade

Full shade

Alpine Forget-Me-Not
(Eritrichium nanum)

DESCRIPTION 6–12 inch (15–30.5 cm) tall flower

HARDY ZONES 3–6

PLANT Plant seeds in fall.

SPACE 6 inches (15 cm)

CARE Water moderately.

DISEASES/PESTS Forget-me-nots are pest- and disease-resistant.

OTHER SPECIES Virginia forget-me-not, tufted forget-me-not

POINT OF FACT Alpine forget-me-nots are native to the western United States and have been Alaska's state flower since 1949.

I GREW IT!

WHEN I GREW IT
DATE

NOTES

VINE

American Wisteria
(Wisteria frutescens)

DESCRIPTION A native vine growing 15–30 feet (4.5–9 m), with showy, fragrant flowers

HARDY ZONES 5–9

PLANT Plant young wisteria or grow from cuttings. Flowers will appear in 2–3 years.

SPACE 4–8 feet (1–2 m)

CARE Water moderately until established. Then prune yearly to control the vine and encourage blooms. Add fertilizer in the spring.

DISEASES/PESTS American wisteria has no serious disease or pest concerns. If flowers fail to appear, assess pruning, fertilizing, and sunlight.

OTHER SPECIES Kentucky wisteria

POINT OF FACT American wisteria is an alternative to the more aggressive Chinese wisteria (*Wisteria sinensis*), which is considered invasive in some states.

I GREW IT!

WHEN I GREW IT
DATE

NOTES

....

....

323

PERENNIAL
Aster
(Symphyotrichum anomalum)

DESCRIPTION 2.5–3 foot (76–91 cm) tall flower in colors pink, purple, blue, and white

HARDY ZONES 3–8

PLANT Plant seeds or seedlings after the last frost.

SPACE 2.5 feet (76 cm)

CARE Water moderately.

DISEASES/PESTS Use a potato trap for slugs and snails.

VARIETIES/CULTIVARS Raydon's favorite, fireworks, purple dome

POINT OF FACT Asters are North American wildflowers. Asters are a September birth flower.

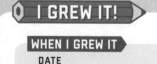

I GREW IT!

WHEN I GREW IT
DATE

NOTES

....

....

Black-eyed Susan
(Rudbeckia hirta)

DESCRIPTION 2–3 foot (61–91 cm) tall plant with yellow or orange flowers

HARDY ZONES 3–7

PLANT Plant seeds or seedlings after the last frost.

SPACE 2 feet (61 cm)

CARE Water heavily; allow to self-seed; divide every 4 years.

DISEASES/PESTS Use an antifungal spray to treat disease.

VARIETIES/CULTIVARS Goldstrum, Maya, prairie sun

POINT OF FACT Black-eyed Susan is native to North America. The flower is named for the poem "Black-Eyed Susan," about a woman in love with a sailor named Sweet William—also the name of a flower.

I GREW IT!

WHEN I GREW IT
DATE

NOTES

....

....

Bleeding Heart

(Lamprocapnos spectabilis)

 to

DESCRIPTION 2–3 foot (61–91 cm) tall plant with drooping heart-shaped flowers

HARDY ZONES 3–9

PLANT Plant from division or seedling after the last frost, or seeds in the fall.

SPACE 3 feet (91 cm)

CARE Water heavily in summer; the plant is short-lived and will be dormant late summer—early spring.

DISEASES/PESTS Spray off aphids.

VARIETIES/CULTIVARS Alba, gold heart, Dutchman's breeches

POINT OF FACT Bleeding hearts are native to northern Asia and prefer cooler temperatures. Bleeding hearts are usually heart-shaped, but the Dutchman's Breeches variety looks like upside-down pants.

I GREW IT!

WHEN I GREW IT
DATE

NOTES

Butterfly Weed
(Asclepias tuberosa)

DESCRIPTION A native wildflower, 1–3 feet (30.5–91 cm) tall and with round cluster flowers

HARDY ZONES 3–9

PLANT Plant seeds after the last frost.

SPACE 12 inches (30.5 cm)

CARE Water seeds regularly. Once plants are established, water only in times of drought.

DISEASES/PESTS Butterfly weeds are mostly disease- and pest-resistant.

VARIETIES/CULTIVARS Western Gold Mix, Hello Yellow, Gay Butterflies

POINT OF FACT Monarch butterfly caterpillars survive mainly on butterfly weed.

I GREW IT!

WHEN I GREW IT
DATE

NOTES

....

....

Buttonbush
(Cephalanthus occidentalis)

DESCRIPTION 5–12 foot (1.5–3.5 m) tall wildflower shrub with flowers that look like pincushions

HARDY ZONES 5–9

PLANT Plant young buttonbushes in spring or fall.

SPACE 4–8 feet (1–2 m)

CARE Water heavily or plant in a low-lying, wet part of the garden.

DISEASES/PESTS Buttonbushes are immune to most diseases and pests.

VARIETIES/CULTIVARS Fiber optics, sugar shack

POINT OF FACT Buttonbushes attract butterflies and are a native alternative to butterfly bush. The flowers bloom in June, gradually harden, and remain intact throughout the winter.

I GREW IT!

WHEN I GREW IT
DATE

NOTES

Camellia
(Camellia)

DESCRIPTION A genus of subtropical plants 6–15 feet (2–4.5 m) tall with glossy leaves and flowers

HARDY ZONES 7–10

PLANT Plant seedlings from late fall to early spring. Add a layer of mulch to preserve moisture.

SPACE 5–10 feet (1.5–3 m)

CARE Water moderately until established, and then lightly.

DISEASES/PESTS Spray off pests such as aphids and thrips.

VARIETIES/CULTIVARS Shiro-wabisuke, Francis Hanger, elegans

POINT OF FACT Camellias are native to east and south Asia. There are over 3,000 camellia hybrids.

I GREW IT!

WHEN I GREW IT
DATE

NOTES

329

BIENNIAL

Common Daisy

(Bellis perennis)

DESCRIPTION 3–6 inch (7.5–15 cm) tall flower

HARDY ZONES 3–7

PLANT Plant seeds in the fall, but do not bury. They need sunlight to germinate.

SPACE 1 foot (30.5 cm)

CARE Water moderately.

DISEASES/PESTS Daisies have no major pests or diseases.

OTHER SPECIES Shasta and gerbera daisies

POINT OF FACT The name means "day's eye" for the way their petals open in the morning.

I GREW IT!

WHEN I GREW IT
DATE

NOTES

....

....

Cosmos
(Cosmos bipinnatus)

DESCRIPTION 1–5 foot (0.5–1.5 m) tall flower

HARDY ZONES 2–11

PLANT Plant seeds 1 week before last frost date.

SPACE 1 foot (30.5 cm)

CARE Water moderately to lightly.

DISEASES/PESTS Spray off aphids; remove plants affected by fungi.

VARIETIES/CULTIVARS Sensation, choco mocha, bright lights

POINT OF FACT Cosmos is known for being a good starter flower for new gardeners. Cosmos is in the aster family, in which each "petal" is an individual flower.

I GREW IT!

WHEN I GREW IT
DATE

NOTES

Daffodil

(Narcissus)

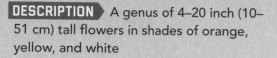

DESCRIPTION A genus of 4–20 inch (10–51 cm) tall flowers in shades of orange, yellow, and white

HARDY ZONES 3–9

PLANT Plant bulbs in the fall.

SPACE 6 inches (15 cm)

CARE Water moderately. Cut back stems in fall. If flowers are no longer blooming well, divide the daffodil bulbs.

DISEASES/PESTS Daffodils are usually pest- and disease-free.

VARIETIES/CULTIVARS Golden ducat, petit four, Rip van Winkle

POINT OF FACT Daffodils are toxic to humans and pets. The botanical name refers to the Greek myth in which a boy falls in love with his own reflection.

◎ I GREW IT!

WHEN I GREW IT
DATE

NOTES

....

....

Daylily
(Hemerocallis)

DESCRIPTION A genus of large flowers, standing 1–3 feet (30.5–91 cm) tall

HARDY ZONES 3–9

PLANT Plant roots in the fall, burying the crown but not packing the soil down over it.

SPACE 24 inches (61 cm)

CARE Water moderately and divide every 4 years.

DISEASES/PESTS Daylilies are susceptible to rust.

VARIETIES/CULTIVARS Adams Street, Arabian magic, atoll

POINT OF FACT Daylilies are not in the lily family. Daylilies symbolize motherhood in China.

 **I GREW IT!**

WHEN I GREW IT
DATE

NOTES

....

....

PERENNIAL

Dogwood

(Cornus florida)

DESCRIPTION 25-foot (7.5 m) tall flowering trees
NOTE: The dogwood fruit will cause an upset stomach if ingested.

HARDY ZONES 5–9

PLANT Plant saplings in spring or summer.

SPACE 20 feet (6 m)

CARE Water moderately till established, and then dogwoods will grow well on their own.

DISEASES/PESTS Dogwood Anthracnose causes brown spots on leaves and flowers. Remove affected parts.

VARIETIES/CULTIVARS apple blossom, white cloud

POINT OF FACT The white "flowers" of a dogwood are actually specialized leaves called bracts, which surround the tiny yellow-green flowers.

I GREW IT!

WHEN I GREW IT
DATE

NOTES

....

....

Eastern Redbud

(Cercis canadensis)

DESCRIPTION 20–30 foot (6–9 m) deciduous flowering tree native to the eastern United States and Canada

HARDY ZONES 4–9

PLANT Plant saplings in early spring.

SPACE 12–15 feet (3.5–4.5 m)

CARE Water moderately until established. Add a layer of mulch around the tree to retain moisture and add new mulch annually.

DISEASES/PESTS Redbuds are most commonly affected by wood borers or canker diseases. Canker diseases are characterized by diseased areas of bark that grow. Cut off affected branches immediately. Wood borers can be destroyed by insecticide, though it is not always effective.

VARIETIES/CULTIVARS Forest pansy, burgundy hearts, covey

POINT OF FACT George Washington transplanted seedlings from the forest into his garden and would write about their beauty in his diary. The redbud is the state tree of Oklahoma.

◗ I GREW IT! ▶

WHEN I GREW IT
DATE

NOTES

....

....

ANNUAL

English Bluebell

(Hyacinthoides non-scripta)

○ to ●

DESCRIPTION 1–1.5 foot (30.5–45.5 cm) tall plant with bell-shaped flowers

HARDY ZONES 4–9

PLANT Plant bulbs in the fall.

SPACE 1 foot (30.5 cm)

CARE Water moderately; divide bulbs every 3 years.

DISEASES/PESTS Spray off aphids.

OTHER SPECIES Spanish bluebells

POINT OF FACT It is illegal to pick bluebells in England. Bluebell sap was used during the Bronze Age as glue to stick feathers to arrows.

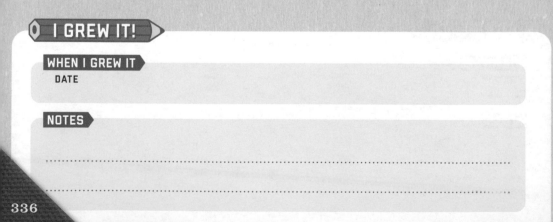

◆ I GREW IT!

WHEN I GREW IT
DATE

NOTES

Foxglove
(Digitalis)

DESCRIPTION A genus of 2–6 foot (0.5–2 m) tall stalks with several bell-shaped flowers

HARDY ZONES 4–10

PLANT Plant seeds after the last frost. They will flower in the second year.

SPACE 2 feet (61 cm)

CARE Water moderately. You can either allow wilted flowers to self-seed or cut them back at the base of the stems so that they grow the next year.

DISEASES/PESTS Foxgloves have no serious pest or disease problems.

VARIETIES/CULTIVARS Candy mountain, mountains mixed, and rose shades

POINT OF FACT Foxgloves attract hummingbirds.

I GREW IT!

WHEN I GREW IT
DATE

NOTES

....

....

Gardenia
(Gardenia)

DESCRIPTION ▶ A genus of evergreen flowering shrubs, 2–8 feet (0.5–2.5 m) tall

HARDY ZONES ▶ 7–11, or as a houseplant

PLANT ▶ Plant seedlings in spring or fall.

SPACE ▶ 3–6 feet (1–2 m)

CARE ▶ Water moderately. Add a layer of mulch where hot, dry summers are common. Prune dead flowers after the blooming season.

DISEASES/PESTS ▶ Spray off small pests, such as whiteflies and mealybugs.

VARIETIES/CULTIVARS ▶ Shooting star, Miami supreme, August beauty

POINT OF FACT ▶ Gardenias were named after Alexander Garden, a Scottish doctor who resided in South Carolina. Gardenias are in the same family as coffee trees.

◖ **I GREW IT!** ▷

WHEN I GREW IT
DATE

NOTES

....

....

Geranium
(Pelargonium)

DESCRIPTION A genus of flowering plants and shrubs

HARDY ZONES 10–11, or as an annual or houseplant in lower zones

PLANT Plant young plants in a pot after the first frost.

SPACE 2 feet (61 cm) or more

CARE Water moderately to lightly. Before the first frost, bring them indoors as a houseplant or put them in a dark spot over winter. They will come back in the spring.

DISEASES/PESTS Treat fungus with fungicide.

VARIETIES/CULTIVARS Summer showers, big red hybrid, citronella

POINT OF FACT Scented geraniums repel insects.

◊ I GREW IT!

WHEN I GREW IT
DATE

NOTES

....

....

Gladiolus
(Gladiolus)

DESCRIPTION A genus of flowers growing tall (1.5–6 feet (0.5–2 m)) and thin

HARDY ZONES 7–10

PLANT Plant corms (the underground stem, similar to a bulb, that stores nutrients and from which the rest of the plant emerges) after the last frost.

SPACE 2 feet (61 cm)

CARE Water moderately. If you are in zone 6 or lower, dig up corms before the first frost. Cut off foliage. Separate the corms, and allow them to dry. Then store in a cool, dry place and replant in the spring.

DISEASES/PESTS Gladiolus are susceptible to gray mold, spider mites, aphids, and rot.

VARIETIES/CULTIVARS Candyman, Prins Claus, black star

POINT OF FACT Gladiola is the August birth flower. The plural of gladiolus is gladioli.

I GREW IT!

WHEN I GREW IT
DATE

NOTES

Globeflower
(Trollius)

to

DESCRIPTION A genus of flowers growing 24 inches (61 cm) tall and thriving along streams and ponds

HARDY ZONES 3–6

PLANT Plant by division or seeds in autumn.

SPACE 1–2 feet (30.5–61cm)

CARE Water heavily and cut off dead flowers.

DISEASES/PESTS Globeflowers are mostly disease free.

VARIETIES/CULTIVARS Earliest of all, goldquelle, canary bird

POINT OF FACT The American globeflower can grow in both mountainous and swampy habitats. The Latin name *trollius* means troll, referring to the flower's round shape.

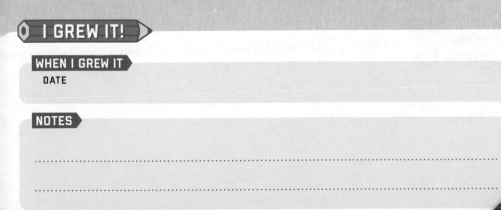

I GREW IT!

WHEN I GREW IT
DATE

NOTES

....

....

Hosta
(Hosta)

 to

DESCRIPTION A genus of shade-loving plants with wide leaves and delicate flowers

HARDY ZONES 3–8

PLANT Plant from division in early spring in moist soil.

SPACE 1–2 feet (30.5–61 cm)

CARE Water moderately to heavily.

DISEASES/PESTS Trap snails and slugs with potato pieces.

VARIETIES/CULTIVARS Love Pat, ground master, hadspen blue

POINT OF FACT Hostas are edible—their young shoots are used in Japanese cooking. Hostas are native to northeast Asia.

I GREW IT!

WHEN I GREW IT
DATE

NOTES

....

....

SHRUB, TREE, VINE

Hydrangea
(Hydrangea)

DESCRIPTION A genus of flowering plants, best known for its 2–15 foot (0.5–4.5 m) tall shrubs

HARDY ZONES 4–9

PLANT Plant seedlings in spring or fall.

SPACE 5 feet (1.5 m)

CARE Water moderately to heavily. Fertilize in the spring.

DISEASES/PESTS Hydrangeas do not have serious pest or disease problems.

VARIETIES/CULTIVARS Grandiflora, Annabelle, snow queen

POINT OF FACT A hydrangea's color depends on the pH of the soil.

WHEN I GREW IT
DATE

NOTES

....

....

PERENNIAL

Impatiens or Bizzy Lizzy
(Impatiens walleriana)

DESCRIPTION ▶ 6 inch–2 foot (15–61 cm) tall and wide flowers

HARDY ZONES ▶ 10–11, or as an annual

PLANT ▶ Plant seedlings after the last frost.

SPACE ▶ 1 foot (30.5 cm)

CARE ▶ Water moderately.

DISEASES/PESTS ▶ Spray off spider mites and whiteflies; pick off caterpillars.

VARIETIES/CULTIVARS ▶ Mini-Hawaiian, jewel, African queen

POINT OF FACT ▶ *Impatiens* is Latin for *impatient*, referring to how quickly the seeds are ejected from the pods.

I GREW IT!

WHEN I GREW IT
DATE

NOTES

....

....

Lilac

(Syringa vulgaris)

DESCRIPTION ▷ A deciduous shrub grown for its clusters of fragrant purple flowers. Lilacs will grow to about 15 feet tall (4.5 m).

HARDY ZONES 3–7

PLANT ▷ Plant seedlings or suckers in spring or fall.

SPACE ▷ 4–6 feet (1–2 m)

CARE ▷ Water lightly and add a fresh layer of compost every spring.

DISEASES/PESTS ▷ Spray pests with water. Avoid blight and mildew by ensuring well-draining soil.

VARIETIES/CULTIVARS ▷ President Grevy, President Lincoln, scent and sensibility

POINT OF FACT ▷ Lilacs are in the olive family and are native to the Mediterranean region. Lilacs are a symbol of first love.

 **I GREW IT!**

WHEN I GREW IT
DATE

NOTES

....

....

Lily of the Valley

(Convallaria majalis)

DESCRIPTION ▸ A spreading flower 1 foot (30.5 cm) tall with narrow leaves and small bell-shaped white flowers that give off a sweet scent

HARDY ZONES ▸ 2–7

PLANT ▸ Plant rhizomes in late fall.

SPACE ▸ 1–2 inches (2.5–5 cm)

CARE ▸ Water moderately.

DISEASES/PESTS ▸ Spray off spider mites and aphids.

VARIETIES/CULTIVARS ▸ Fortin's giant, rosea

POINT OF FACT ▸ Lily of the valley is not related to other lilies. Lily of the valley has been used in perfume and medicine.

I GREW IT!

WHEN I GREW IT
DATE

NOTES

Magnolia
(Magnolia)

DESCRIPTION A genus of evergreen flowering trees found in warm climates around the world and ranging in height from 8 to 80 feet (2.5–24 m)

HARDY ZONES 6–10, depending on the variety

PLANT Plant saplings in early spring.

SPACE 15–20 feet (4.5–6 m)

CARE Water moderately until established.

DISEASES/PESTS Magnolias are disease- and pest-resistant.

VARIETIES/CULTIVARS Exmouth, norman gould, Wakehurst

POINT OF FACT Known as the Magnolia state, Mississippi has named magnolias their official state flower. Magnolias are often pollinated by beetles who use the pollen as a protein source.

I GREW IT!

WHEN I GREW IT
DATE

NOTES

....

....

347

Marigold
(Tagetes)

DESCRIPTION A genus of 6–12 inch (15–30.5 cm) tall flowers with colors ranging from red to yellow

HARDY ZONES 2–11

PLANT Plant seedlings after the last frost.

SPACE 12 inches (30.5 cm)

CARE Water moderately. Deadhead blooms.

DISEASES/PESTS Spray off aphids.

VARIETIES/CULTIVARS Gold coin, Janie, hero

POINT OF FACT In the 1960s, marigolds were passed over for roses to be named the national flower. Native to Mexico, marigolds are popular altar flowers for Dia de los Muertos.

I GREW IT!

WHEN I GREW IT
DATE

NOTES

....

....

Peony
(Paeonia lactiflora)

DESCRIPTION Flowering perennials 2–4 feet (61–122 cm) tall. (Shrub species can grow taller.)

HARDY ZONES 3–8

PLANT In the fall, plant rhizomes with buds facing up.

SPACE 3–4 feet (91–122 cm)

CARE Water lightly.

DISEASES/PESTS Peonies are disease- and pest-resistant. Spray off any small pests.

VARIETIES/CULTIVARS Bowl of Beauty, Festiva Maxima, Sarah Bernhardt

POINT OF FACT Peonies can live for over 100 years. Ants are attracted to the nectar of peonies. They neither harm the plants, nor, contrary to popular belief, do the work of opening the flowers.

I GREW IT!

WHEN I GREW IT
DATE

NOTES

....

....

Petunia

(Petunia)

 to

DESCRIPTION A genus of 12-inch (30.5 cm) tall or long flowers that comes in all colors and is often vining

HARDY ZONES 9–11, or as an annual

PLANT Plant seedlings after the last frost.

SPACE 12 inches (30.5 cm)

CARE Water lightly; deadhead blooms.

DISEASES/PESTS Spray off aphids, and pick off caterpillars.

VARIETIES/CULTIVARS Supercascade, fancy dress, black cat

POINT OF FACT Petunias originated in South America. The types available are known as hybrids—a cross between more than one species.

◖ I GREW IT! ▻

WHEN I GREW IT
DATE

NOTES

....

....

SHRUB

Poinsettia
(Euphorbia pulcherrima)

to

DESCRIPTION A shrub 3–10 feet (1–3 m) tall, with green and red, pink, or cream leaves, and often kept as a smaller houseplant

HARDY ZONES 9–11, or indoors in a pot

PLANT Plant a small poinsettia after Christmas in warm climates. For a potted plant, allow it to go dormant after blooming. In March, repot the plant, place it in a sunny window, and cut it back to 6 inches (15 cm).

SPACE 3–7 feet (1–2 m)

CARE Water moderately.

DISEASES/PESTS To avoid scab, gray mold, and mildew, ensure well-draining soil.

VARIETIES/CULTIVARS candy cane, sparkling punch, lilo pink

POINT OF FACT Poinsettias are popular Christmas gifts. The bright red so-called "flowers" are modified leaves, whereas the real flowers are small and yellow.

 **I GREW IT!**

WHEN I GREW IT
DATE

NOTES

351

Primrose
(Primula polyanthus)

DESCRIPTION Flowering perennials that are low-growing and spreading

HARDY ZONES 5–7

PLANT Plant seeds or seedlings in spring or fall.

SPACE 6–12 inches (15–30.5 cm)

CARE Water moderately.

DISEASES/PESTS Trap slugs and snails; spray off spider mites and aphids.

VARIETIES/CULTIVARS Gold laced group

POINT OF FACT The name primrose came from the Latin *prima rosa*, meaning first flower. Besides this one, there are 500 to 600 species of primrose.

I GREW IT!

WHEN I GREW IT
DATE

NOTES

SHRUB

Rhododendron
(Rhododendron)

to

DESCRIPTION A genus of evergreen shrubs 4–6 feet (1–2 m) tall

HARDY ZONES 5–8

PLANT Plant seedlings in late spring or early fall. Add a layer of mulch to preserve moisture.

SPACE 4–6 feet (1–2 m)

CARE Water moderately until established, and then lightly. Replace mulch annually.

DISEASES/PESTS Azaleas are disease- and pest-resistant.

VARIETIES/CULTIVARS Elvira, blue peter, bow bells

POINT OF FACT The genus *Rhododendron* is one of the largest in the plant kingdom. Azaleas are a popular kind of rhododendron.

WHEN I GREW IT
DATE

NOTES

....

....

SHRUB
Rose
(Rosa)

 to

DESCRIPTION A genus of flowering shrubs and vines, usually around 4 feet (1 m) tall, but capable of growing much taller

HARDY ZONES 5–9

PLANT Plant young roses after the last frost or in early fall. Wear gloves and long sleeves to avoid being pricked by thorns. Place bonemeal at the bottom of the hole for best results.

SPACE Depends on the variety

CARE Water moderately; prune before it wilts to encourage new growth.

DISEASES/PESTS Spray off small pests with water. Provide good air circulation and well-draining soil to prevent mildew and rust. Remove diseased parts of the plant if afflicted.

VARIETIES/CULTIVARS Bonica, teasing Georgia, rainbow knockout

POINT OF FACT Roses are edible and are actually a great source of vitamin C. Thought to be the oldest rose in the world, the rose of Hildesheim is more than 1,000 years old. It is protected at its base by an iron fence.

I GREW IT!

WHEN I GREW IT
DATE

NOTES

....

....

ANNUAL
Sunflower
(Helianthus)

DESCRIPTION A genus of plants, mostly native to North and Central America, having 1–15 foot (30.5 cm–4.5 m) tall stalks with large flowers that produce edible seeds

HARDY ZONES 2–11

PLANT Plant after the last frost, 1 inch (2.5 cm) apart. Thin once there are 2 leaves.

SPACE 6 inches apart (15 cm)

CARE Water heavily when young, and then lightly.

DISEASES/PESTS Sunflowers are disease- and pest-resistant. The seeds attract birds as they dry and fall.

VARIETIES/CULTIVARS titan, teddy bear, sunny smile

POINT OF FACT The sunflower bloom follows the movements of the sun. Sunflowers are the state flower of Kansas but listed as a noxious weed in Iowa.

 **I GREW IT!**

WHEN I GREW IT
DATE

NOTES

....
....
....

Texas Bluebonnet

(Lupinus texensis)

DESCRIPTION 2-foot (61 cm) tall plants with blue flower clusters

HARDY ZONES 6–8

PLANT Plant seeds in fall. First soak seeds for 2 days. Then plant by scattering on the soil and walking over the space to bury the seeds.

SPACE 1 foot (30.5 cm)

CARE Water lightly. Allow flowers to wilt so that they reseed themselves and grow again in the spring.

DISEASES/PESTS Insects and birds might try to eat the bluebonnet flowers. Bluebonnets are susceptible to fungal diseases.

OTHER SPECIES sandyland or Big Bend

POINT OF FACT Bluebonnets are the state flower of Texas. They grow as a wildflower but are also planted along roadsides.

I GREW IT!

WHEN I GREW IT
DATE

NOTES

Tulip
(Tulipa)

DESCRIPTION > A genus of bulb flowers 4–28 inches (10–71 cm) tall

HARDY ZONES > 3–8

PLANT > Plant bulbs 6 inches (15 cm) deep in autumn.

SPACE > 6 inches (15 cm)

CARE > Water lightly. Add fertilizer or compost to the soil for best results. Divide in the fall.

DISEASES/PESTS > Remove any plants afflicted with fungi.

VARIETIES/CULTIVARS > Single early, double early, triumph

POINT OF FACT > The Netherlands is the number one tulip-producing country in the world. Tulip petals are edible and taste like onions.

I GREW IT!

WHEN I GREW IT >
DATE

NOTES

....

....

Western Wallflower
(*Erysimum capitatum*)

DESCRIPTION 1–2 foot (30.5–61 cm) tall flower with orange and yellow blooms

HARDY ZONES 3–7

PLANT Plant seeds in the fall or early spring. Broadcast seeds and walk over to bury.

SPACE 1 foot (30.5 cm)

CARE Water lightly and allow to self-seed.

DISEASES/PESTS Treat gray mold with fungicide.

OTHER SPECIES coastal wallflower, European wallflower

POINT OF FACT The Western wallflower is a North American wildflower that grows on rocky terrain. It was named after its European relatives, which really do grow on walls.

I GREW IT!

WHEN I GREW IT
DATE

NOTES

....

....

Zinnia
(Zinnia elegans)

DESCRIPTION 1–4 foot (30.5–122 cm) tall flower in a variety of colors

HARDY ZONES 2–11

PLANT Plant seeds after the last frost.

SPACE 1 foot (30.5 cm)

CARE Water moderately; deadhead flowers.

DISEASES/PESTS Pick off caterpillars, and spray off smaller insects.

VARIETIES/CULTIVARS Thumbelina, envy, state fair

POINT OF FACT Zinnias attract butterflies. Zinnias are native to the US Southwest, Mexico, and Central America.

 I GREW IT!

WHEN I GREW IT
DATE

NOTES

....

....

SUCCULENT GUIDE

In warm, dry climates, succulents are perfect for the garden. Elsewhere, they can be grown as houseplants and moved outdoors in the summer.

LIGHT NEEDS

 Full sun

 Partial sun

 Partial shade

 Full shade

PARRY'S AGAVE

COPPER KING/LADYFINGER

SPINYSTAR

CHOCOLATE SOLDIER

African Candelabra

(Euphorbia ammak)

DESCRIPTION 15–30 foot (4.5–9 m) tall cactus that branches out like a candelabra

HARDY ZONES 9–11, or as a houseplant

NOTE: The hotter the climate, the more shade needed.

PLANT Plant small plants or cuttings in the ground or in pots.

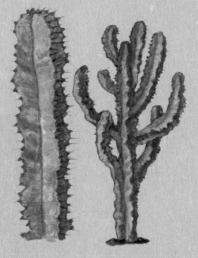

SPACE 6–12 feet (2–3.5 m)

CARE Water lightly.

DISEASES/PESTS Brush or spray off pests.

OTHER SPECIES Crown-of-Thorns, baseball plant, coral cactus

POINT OF FACT It is native to Saudi Arabia and Yemen. In the spring, yellow-green flowers produce inedible green fruit.

◖ I GREW IT! ▷

WHEN I GREW IT
DATE

NOTES

....

....

Balloon Cactus
(Parodia magnifica)

DESCRIPTION 6–12 inch (15–30.5 cm) tall and wide cactus that grows in clusters in the ground, but often as a single plant in a pot

HARDY ZONES 9–11, or as a houseplant

PLANT Plant a young cactus or seed in the ground or in a pot.

SPACE 1 foot (30.5 cm)

CARE Water lightly. Repot every 3 years, potting up if needed.

DISEASES/PESTS Spray or brush off small insects.

OTHER SPECIES Parodia buiningii, parodia rutilans

POINT OF FACT The older the balloon cactus gets, the bluer it becomes.

I GREW IT!

WHEN I GREW IT
DATE

NOTES

....

....

Blue Chalk Sticks

(Senecio mandraliscae)

DESCRIPTION 1–2 foot (30.5–61 cm) tall succulent with blue-green finger-shaped leaves growing from thick stems.

HARDY ZONES 9–11, or as a houseplant

PLANT Plant young succulent in the ground or in a pot.

SPACE 3 feet (91 cm)

CARE Water lightly.

DISEASES/PESTS Brush or spray off small pests.

OTHER SPECIES Angel wings, spearhead, trident blue, fishhooks

POINT OF FACT Blue Senecio is a popular border plant in warm regions. It is native to southern Africa.

I GREW IT!

WHEN I GREW IT
DATE

NOTES

Chocolate Soldier

(Kalanchoe tomentosa)

DESCRIPTION 1–3 feet (30.5–91 cm) tall and wide succulent with fuzzy leaves tipped reddish brown

HARDY ZONES 9–12, or as a houseplant

PLANT Plant young succulents or cuttings in the ground or in a pot.

SPACE 3 feet (91 cm)

CARE Water lightly.

DISEASES/PESTS No major pests.

OTHER SPECIES Snow white panda plant, yellow kalanchoe, Christmas tree plant

POINT OF FACT Chocolate soldiers are a sign of wealth and prosperity. The plant is native to Madagascar.

◎ I GREW IT!

WHEN I GREW IT
DATE

NOTES

....
....
....

Copper King/Ladyfinger

(Mammillaria elongata)

DESCRIPTION 8-inch (20.5 cm) cylindrical cactus that grows in clusters

HARDY ZONES 9–11, or as a houseplant

PLANT Plant a young cactus, seed, or cutting in the ground or a small pot.

SPACE 3–9 inches (7.5–23 cm)

CARE Water lightly.

DISEASES/PESTS Use fungicide for infections.

OTHER SPECIES Old lady cactus, powder puff, feather cactus

POINT OF FACT Many *Mammillaria* species have soft, hairy spines.

I GREW IT!

WHEN I GREW IT
DATE

NOTES

....

....

Golden Barrel Cactus

(Echinocactus grusonii)

DESCRIPTION A ball-shaped cactus with long sharp spines, usually growing 2–3 feet (61–91 cm) tall and wide

HARDY ZONES 9–11, or as a houseplant

PLANT Plant a small cactus in the ground or in a pot.

SPACE 3 feet (91 cm)

CARE Water lightly.

DISEASES/PESTS Spray or brush off small pests.

OTHER SPECIES Devil's pincushion, devil's head

POINT OF FACT Though a popular cactus in private and public gardens alike, the golden barrel cactus is endangered in the wild.

◖ I GREW IT! ▷

WHEN I GREW IT
DATE

NOTES

....
....
....

Indian Fig Prickly Pear
(Opuntia ficus-indica)

DESCRIPTION 6–20 foot (2–6 m) tall cactus with pads and fruit used in food and medicine

HARDY ZONES 9–11, or as a houseplant

PLANT Plant a pad in the ground in hot, dry climates or in a pot with cactus and potting mix. Pot up each year.

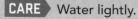

SPACE 5 feet (1.5 m)

CARE Water lightly.

DISEASES/PESTS Prickly pears are fairly disease- and pest-resistant.

OTHER SPECIES *Opuntia humifusa, Opuntia cacanapa, Opuntia microdasys*

POINT OF FACT Flowers bloom each spring or summer, giving way to sweet fruit. Nopales—the pads of the prickly pear cactus—are high in vitamin C, calcium, and magnesium.

I GREW IT!

WHEN I GREW IT

DATE

NOTES

PERENNIAL
Jellybean
(Sedum rubrotinctum)

DESCRIPTION 6–12 inch (15–30.5 cm) trailing succulent with jellybean-shaped leaves

HARDY ZONES 9–11, or as a houseplant

PLANT Plant a young succulent or cutting outdoors in hot, dry climates or in a pot with cactus and potting mix.

SPACE 1 foot (30.5 cm)

CARE Water lightly indoors, not at all outdoors.

DISEASES/PESTS None.

OTHER SPECIES Two-row stonecrop, Corsican stonecrop, woodland stonecrop

POINT OF FACT Its other nickname, pork and beans, refers to the leaves turning brownish red in the summer.

I GREW IT!

WHEN I GREW IT
DATE

NOTES

Parry's Agave
(Agave parryi)

DESCRIPTION 2-foot (61 cm) tall and wide grayish-blue succulent native to the southwestern United States and northern Mexico

HARDY ZONES 5–11

PLANT Plant small succulent outdoors in very dry climates or in a 15-gallon (56.5 L) pot filled with part cactus mix and part potting mix. Avoid transplanting.

SPACE 2 feet (61 cm)

CARE Water lightly.

DISEASES/PESTS Scale, slugs, and snails can afflict *Agave parryi*. These can be repelled with soapy water, blown or sprayed off, or picked off.

OTHER SPECIES Century agave, Queen Elizabeth agave, blue agave

POINT OF FACT At the end of its 20-year life span, a 15-foot (4.5 m) tall flower stalk emerges and blooms. Native American tribes of the Southwest roasted agave hearts for a sweet treat.

WHEN I GREW IT
DATE

NOTES

Silver Dollar Jade

(Crassula arborescens)

to

DESCRIPTION 4-foot (2 m) tall and 3-foot (91 cm) wide succulent with a woody base and rubbery leaves

HARDY ZONES 9-11, or as a houseplant

PLANT Plant young succulents or cuttings in the ground or in a pot.

SPACE 3 feet (91 cm)

CARE Water lightly.

DISEASES/PESTS Spray or brush off small pests.

OTHER SPECIES Gandalf jade, coral jade, curly jade

POINT OF FACT The silver dollar jade's name comes from its leaves, which grow to roughly the size of a silver dollar. Silver dollar jades are adapted to the strong winds around the Cape of Good Hope, and thus have strong roots.

I GREW IT!

WHEN I GREW IT
DATE

NOTES

Spinystar
(Escobaria vivipara)

DESCRIPTION 1-foot (30.5 cm) or smaller cactus, shaped like a ball and covered thickly with spikes

HARDY ZONES 4–11

PLANT Plant young succulents in the spring, or in a pot with cactus mix and potting mix. Water deeply after planting.

SPACE 1 foot (30.5 cm)

CARE Water lightly.

DISEASES/PESTS Disease- and pest-resistant.

OTHER SPECIES radiosa, rosea, Arizonica

POINT OF FACT Spinystar is one of only 4 cacti that grow wild in Canada. In spring and summer, flowers give way to an edible fruit called tunas.

I GREW IT!

WHEN I GREW IT
DATE

NOTES

1

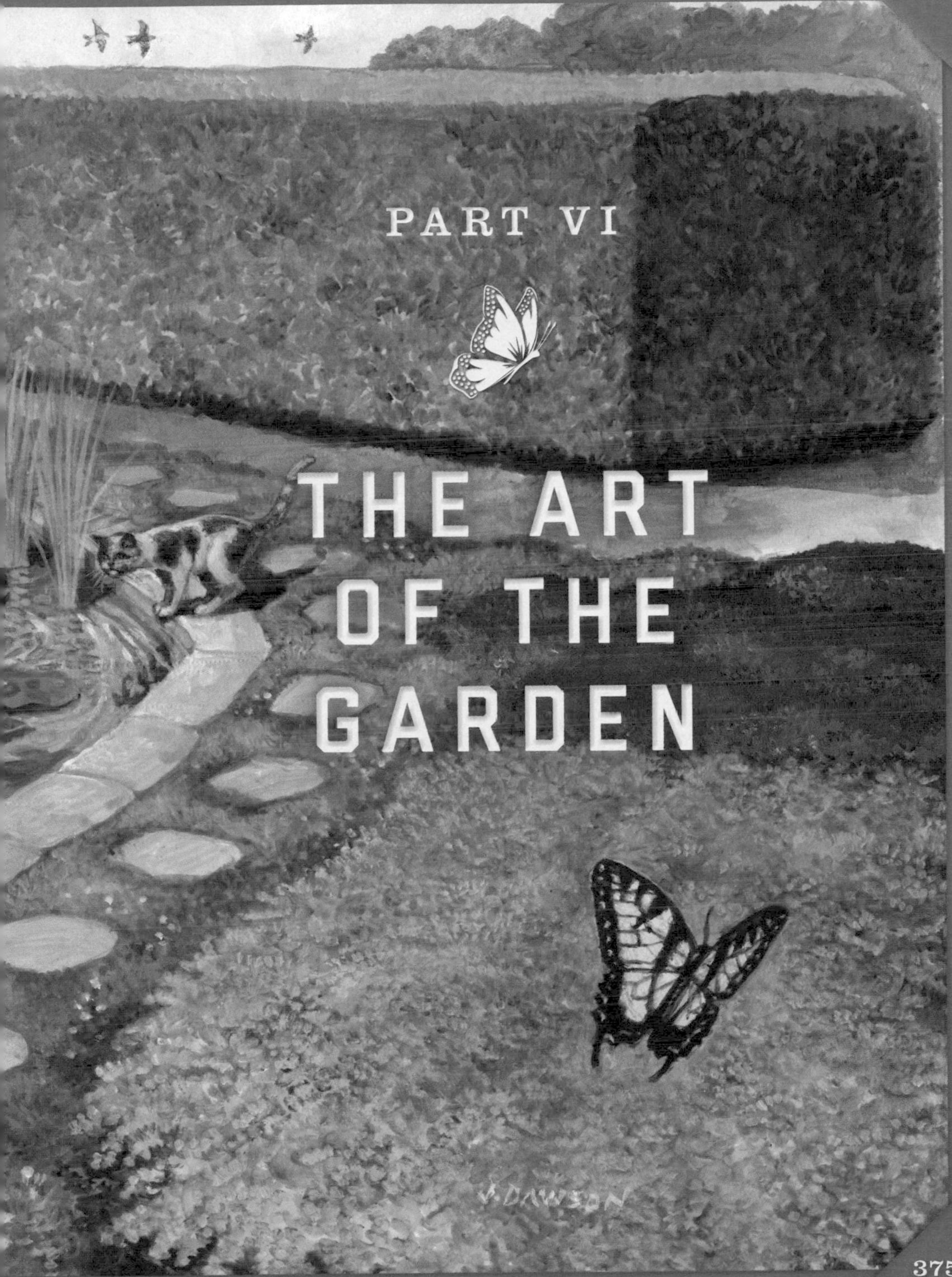

PART VI

THE ART
OF THE
GARDEN

V. DAWSON

What would YOU do?

You are staying with your grandparents

for the summer. Your grandfather is famous for his green thumb. But he has been injured and is unable to tend his garden. You arrive to find overgrown plants and vines. Underneath, you know there are pathways and garden beds of all kinds. You have time on your hands. *What would you do?*

CHAPTER 1

A Garden Paradise

You started small—with a few pots or a single raised bed. Now it's time to think big. Your yard is itself a garden. Every inch of it can be used for beauty and function. It may include pathways, seating areas, water features, and even places to play. Walled gardens—gardens enclosed on all sides—tend to have straight lines, such as four square garden beds divided by a plus-shaped path, and enclosed by walls, hedges, or a fence. Cottage gardens have a more free-form shape: Think flower beds cascading from the house to a picket fence. If you are really thinking big, you might grow a cottage garden in the front yard and a walled garden in the back!

The Walled Garden

Walled gardens date back to ancient times, when they were considered the best places imaginable. In fact, the word paradise comes from the Persian pairidaeza—a wall enclosing a garden. Your yard

probably isn't surrounded by walls. But it likely has built-in perimeters: your home on one side, and perhaps a fence on the other three. Within those structures, you can create a paradise. Common elements include a perimeter, a pathway, plots for plants, structures for vines, focal points such as water features and arches, and places to relax.

TRACK IT ↘   Public Gardens

A public garden is a place where people can visit to learn about plants and relax in the beauty of nature. You may even get ideas for your own garden! The focus of a public garden varies from native plants to rare plants to roses to heirloom plants (often grown alongside a historical home). They may fill acres or only a tiny nook in a public park.

Research public gardens near you or the places you travel. Then plan a visit. Afterward, write the name of the garden and sketch or write notes about what caught your eye.

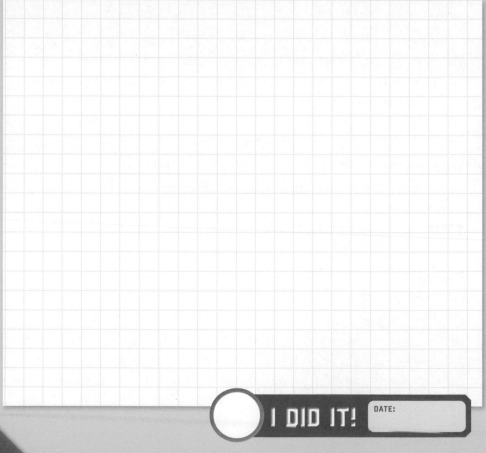

I DID IT!   DATE:

TRY IT →

Grow a Native Hedge

Live in zones 7–10? Wax myrtle is an excellent choice for a native hedge. It is evergreen, fragrant, and bouquet beautiful. Plus, it grows fast: 3–5 feet (1–1.5 m) per year! What more could you want from a hedge?

> **WHAT YOU'LL NEED**
> ➢ 1 wax myrtle plant per 5 feet (1.5 m) of perimeter, a shovel, mulch, and garden shears

STEP 1 Dig a trench slightly wider and deeper than the root ball, and the length of your perimeter.

STEP 2 Set the saplings 5 feet (1.5 m) apart from one another.

STEP 3 Refill with soil. Surround the shrubs with mulch.

STEP 4 Water moderately the first 2 years. Then they will be drought-tolerant in all but desert conditions.

STEP 5 Trim the hedge beginning the second year. You can create a standard wall shape, or something more whimsical.

I DID IT! DATE:

Perimeters and Paths

If you don't already have a perimeter in place, try growing your own living wall. The most wall-like planting is a hedge—shrubs grown closely together.

A pathway encourages people to walk through the garden. If you already have grass growing, that can be the pathway. If your yard is muddy, a simple path can be created with straw or mulch. If you have the resources, stones make beautiful pathways. For a living pathway, intersperse crawling plants such as wooly thyme, creeping Jenny, or blue star creeper between the stones.

Create a Living Pathway

WHAT YOU'LL NEED

➤ pavers, trowel, and crawling plants that can withstand heavy foot traffic, such as wooly thyme, creeping Jenny, or blue star creeper

STEP 1 Create a pathway with the pavers, leaving at least 6 inches (15 cm) in between them.

STEP 2 With the trowel, dig holes just deep enough to bury the seedlings' root balls.

STEP 3 Plant 2–3 seedlings between each stone.

STEP 4 Water weekly the first year. They are drought-tolerant once established.

I DID IT! DATE:

Plots for Plants

A walled garden is usually geometrical. Most yards are rectangular. The plots within are rectangles, squares, and circles. This style is also called a potager, literally meaning soup garden, but is understood to be a beautiful, structured garden that mostly produces food. Start with long rectangular plots along the perimeter. Then add plots inside, with a focal point at the center.

A traditional potager looks something like this.

Structures

A walled garden is all about structure. (Except for the plants, of course, which grow and overflow.) Unfortunately, structures can be expensive or labor-intensive to build. Remember, the garden doesn't have to be perfect. If you can create beautiful raised beds made of wood, stone, or brick, great! But the pathway creates structure enough if your raised beds are no more than mounds of garden soil. You can use the existing fence as scaffolding for vining plants or espalier trees. And then create your own structures with bamboo poles.

A Water Feature

A water feature provides a tranquil focal point in the garden. In it, you can grow water plants and even raise fish. It may also attract birds, butterflies, frogs, and other wildlife. A water garden can be as small as a bowl or as large as a fountain or pond.

A small bowl needs no more than a small solar fountain to stay fresh for a few weeks. The fountain oxygenates the water, preventing the growth of anaerobic bacteria—the smelly kind. It also attracts birds and other wildlife. The trickling sound signals fresh water for drinking and insects hovering in the mist. Alternately, you can float a couple of water plants. These also oxygenate the water and provide shade, slowing algal growth. If you'd like, add a small fish to eat mosquito larvae. Watch the temperature, though. Small bowls can quickly freeze in the winter and get too hot in the summer. Even with plants or fountains, small bowls will need to be emptied and sprayed out every couple of weeks or whenever algae starts to take over.

For a larger water garden, emptying and refilling is impractical, so a filtration system is essential for controlling algae and bad bacteria. Ponds support plants that root at the bottom, floating plants, and shallow water plants. Fish will also be happy in a larger pond, where deep water remains cool in the summer and unfrozen in the winter. Or wait for the inevitable arrival of native frogs, snails, and turtles.

A Place to Rest or Play

Gardens aren't just for working. They're also for enjoying. Every garden should have a place to relax or play. That may be as simple as a hammock or swing. Or you can create something magical.

TRY IT → Make a Simple Water Garden

➢ a 5-gallon (19 L) bowl with no drainage hole, or ono with a plug; 2 floating plants or a small solar fountain; and water

STEP 1 Place the bowl in a spot that has partial shade.

STEP 2 Fill the bowl with water.

STEP 3 Add plants or a fountain.

STEP 4 Change the water every 2 weeks to avoid algae build-up and mosquito development.

I DID IT! DATE:

TAKE IT TO THE NEXT LEVEL ↗

Create a Small Pond

WHAT YOU'LL NEED

➢ a shovel, a pond liner, a filtration system, a fountain or waterfall pump, floating water plants, rooted water plants in pots, and pebbles

STEP 1 Choose a flat spot in partial sun. Place the pond liner in the spot you plan to put it. Mark around it.

STEP 2 Dig out the pond's shape. Also dig a spot for the water filter and waterfall pump if you are using one.

STEP 3 Add the pond liner, water filter, and any other structures, and hook them up according to the directions.

STEP 4 Scatter pebbles along the bottom.

STEP 5 Add water. Power up the water filter and fountain or waterfall.

STEP 6 Sink rooted water plants in their pots or add aquatic plant medium to the bottom of the pond and plant them there.

STEP 7 Add floating plants.

STEP 8 After a month, add fish if you choose.

I DID IT!   DATE:

TRY IT → Make a Natural Living Room

WHAT YOU'LL NEED

➤ shady spot in the garden, stones for the perimeter, shovel or trowel, Irish or Scottish moss, and tree stumps or logs

STEP 1 Choose a shady spot, preferably with little growing there. Line stones around the perimeter.

STEP 2 Plant the moss. Dig a hole every 12 inches (30.5 cm) that is deep enough to bury the roots. Plant the moss. Keep it damp. It will spread in time.

STEP 3 Add tree stumps or logs for seating.

I DID IT! DATE:

TAKE IT TO THE NEXT LEVEL ↗

Grow a Sunflower Fort

Make your own shade and privacy with a sunflower fort.

WHAT YOU'LL NEED
➢ shovel, packet of sunflower seeds, mulch, and outdoor pillows (optional)

STEP 1 Select a sunny spot.

STEP 2 Measure an 8-foot (2 m) diameter circle.

STEP 3 Along the perimeter, dig a trench 1 foot (30.5 cm) deep. Leave 3 feet (91 cm) undug for the entrance. Break up the soil and add fertilizer or compost.

STEP 4 Plant sunflower seeds 6 inches (15 cm) apart and 1 inch (2.5 cm) deep.

STEP 5 As the sunflowers grow and make shade, the grass will suffer. Fill the space with mulch so that it is not muddy.

STEP 6 Add outdoor pillows for seating.

I DID IT! DATE:

A Cottage Garden

Whereas a walled garden is geometrical, a cottage garden is free-flowing. Winding paths, curving garden beds, and spreading flowers and herbs are hallmarks of cottage gardens. It's common for a cottage garden to be in the front yard, where the flowers can be enjoyed by all. However, you can plant it wherever you have the space—surrounding a garage or playhouse, in a quiet corner, or in a sunny side yard. Just don't underestimate the work of a cottage garden. Though it may look casual and accidental, it requires as much planning and time as any other garden.

Where to Begin

With a walled garden, you plant along the perimeters and work your way in. Cottage gardens are built the opposite way. Plant alongside your house and pathway and work your way out. In front of the house, add flowering shrubs and climbing plants, or for a simpler option, overflowing flower boxes and pots. Then make two long garden beds along your front path, garage, or fence. Plant it with perennial and self-seeding flowers and herbs. You can save money by planting seeds, or planting seedlings sparsely. The garden will look bare at first, but the flowers will soon spread and reseed themselves.

What to Grow

In a cottage garden, flowering shrubs, flowers, and herbs delight all who pass by. You might have a cottage garden in the front yard and a walled garden with fruits and vegetables in the back. However, feel free to incorporate fruits and vegetables into your cottage garden. Fruit plants and shrubs fit in especially well because of their fragrant flowers and spreading nature. Here are some key plant types to include:

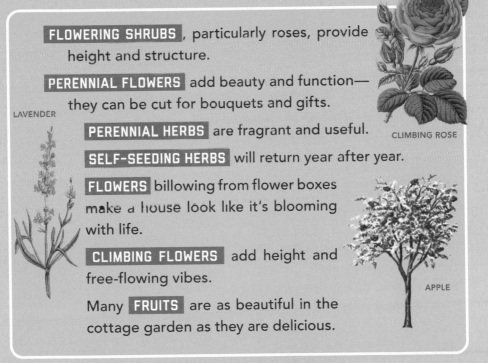

FLOWERING SHRUBS, particularly roses, provide height and structure.

PERENNIAL FLOWERS add beauty and function—they can be cut for bouquets and gifts.

PERENNIAL HERBS are fragrant and useful.

SELF-SEEDING HERBS will return year after year.

FLOWERS billowing from flower boxes make a house look like it's blooming with life.

CLIMBING FLOWERS add height and free-flowing vibes.

Many **FRUITS** are as beautiful in the cottage garden as they are delicious.

LAVENDER

CLIMBING ROSE

APPLE

To incorporate vegetables into a cottage garden, dig out a separate garden plot. That way, when you work the soil each spring, you won't disrupt the perennials.

Compact Cottage Gardens

Not allowed to turn your entire front yard into a cottage garden? Try these smaller cottage garden ideas instead.

Cottage gardens often contain a rustic bench, trellis, or fence. You can create the feel of a cottage garden by surrounding a bench with cottage garden plants.

Create the look of a cottage garden on your front porch with billowing flowers, fragrant herbs, and bursting blooms—all growing in pots and boxes.

If you have a playhouse, create a mini cottage garden just outside. No playhouse? Try it beside a garage or shed.

Maintaining and Expanding

Here's where the work of the perennial garden comes in: As the flowers grow and spread, you'll need to control them so that the garden doesn't become a tangled mess. You'll need to cut back perennials to make room for more growth, divide perennials when they crowd one another, and weed out flowers where they don't belong. That can take hours of work. So, while a perennial garden may seem like a one-time job, it is really an ongoing project.

As you divide perennials and pull up wayward flowers, you can give them away, or make space to replant them. Add garden beds next to the original garden beds, leaving a pathway in between so that you can access the plants.

 **TRY IT →** Grow a Rain Garden

A rain garden is designed to capture rainwater that would otherwise run off into lower parts of your property or a storm drain, causing flooding or pollution. It can double as a native plants garden, thus supporting wildlife at the same time. Situate the rain garden in a naturally low-lying part of your yard or dig a trench for it.

WHAT YOU'LL NEED

➤ a shovel, compost or manure, and native plant seeds or seedlings

STEP 1 If the area is already low-lying, remove the existing vegetation with the shovel. If the ground is level, dig a wide trench.

STEP 2 Work in the compost or manure.

STEP 3 Plant the seeds and seedlings as directed.

STEP 4 Water the plants heavily until they mature. Then they will be able to rely on the rainwater.

 I DID IT! DATE:

HEDGE GUIDE

Hedges add structure to your garden, creating natural walls and fences. Once planted, they require minimal care.

DAPPLED WILLOW

GROUND COVER GUIDE

Ground cover is used to fill empty spaces (preventing weeds) and add shape to your garden. Choose hardy, low-growing plants that are suited to your climate.

CREEPING JENNY

WATER PLANT GUIDE

A pond is a peaceful addition to any garden. Water plants beautify the pond, filter the water, and attract fish and amphibians.

WATER LILY

Dappled Willow
(Salix integra)

 to

DESCRIPTION 4–6 foot (1–2 m) tall shrub with pink-green leaves, giving the appearance of being in bloom

HARDY ZONES 4–9

PLANT Plant saplings in a trench in the spring.

SPACE 3 feet (91 cm)

CARE Water moderately. Prune in late winter every 2–3 years.

DISEASES/PESTS Willows are disease-prone. Spray off small pests. Treat diseases with oils or sprays.

VARIETIES/CULTIVARS Hahuro-Nishiki, flamingo

POINT OF FACT Dappled willows are most colorful in climates with cool summers. Dappled willows lose their leaves in winter, revealing bright red stems.

I GREW IT!

WHEN I GREW IT
DATE

NOTES

English Boxwood
(Buxus sempervirens)

to

DESCRIPTION 5–15 foot (1.5–4.5) tall evergreen shrub with dense foliage

HARDY ZONES 5–8

PLANT Plant saplings in a trench in the spring.

SPACE 2 feet (61 cm)

CARE Add mulch to the base of the bushes. Water moderately.

DISEASES/PESTS No serious disease or pest problems.

VARIETIES/CULTIVARS Appalachian pyramid, Aurea pendula, Chloe

POINT OF FACT Boxwoods grow slower than most hedges, making them easy to maintain. Boxwood is used to make wreaths and other holiday decorations.

I GREW IT!

WHEN I GREW IT
DATE

NOTES

Creeping Jenny

(Lysimachia nummularia)

 to

DESCRIPTION A low-growing, quickly spreading plant with small light green leaves and yellow flowers

NOTE: Creeping Jenny is considered invasive in some states.

HARDY ZONES 3–9

PLANT Plant from divisions or seedlings after the last frost.

SPACE 18 inches (45.5 cm)

CARE Water moderately. Creeping Jenny prefers heavy water, but that can result in aggressive growth. Prune to control.

DISEASES/PESTS Creeping Jenny is disease- and pest-resistant.

VARIETIES/CULTIVARS Aurea

POINT OF FACT Creeping Jenny is also known as moneywort for its coin-shaped leaves. Creeping Jenny makes a good indoor hanging plant.

I GREW IT!

WHEN I GREW IT
DATE

NOTES

PERENNIAL

Irish Moss

(Sagina subulata)

 to

DESCRIPTION 1-inch (2.5 cm) tall spreading plant with emerald-green foliage and small white flowers

HARDY ZONES 4–10

PLANT Plant seeds, cuttings, or young plants. Take clumps of Irish moss and plant them throughout the area you want to cover. Then water deeply. Seeds can be started after the last frost. Scatter seeds and keep wet for up to 3 weeks until they germinate.

SPACE 1 foot (30.5 cm)

CARE Water moderately.

DISEASES/PESTS Pick off slugs.

OTHER SPECIES Scottish Moss

POINT OF FACT Irish moss is not actually in the moss family. True mosses do not flower. Irish moss is also the name of an edible seaweed that grows in the Atlantic Ocean.

 **I GREW IT!**

WHEN I GREW IT
DATE

NOTES

....

....

American Lotus

(Nelumbo lutea)

DESCRIPTION 3–6 foot (1–2 m) tall flower that grows in ponds

HARDY ZONES 4–10

PLANT Plant rhizomes in a pot filled with garden soil (not potting mix, as it will float away). Stems and leaves should remain unburied. Add gravel on top of the soil. Submerge the pot in water 2–3 feet (61–91 cm).

SPACE 1 foot (30.5 cm)

CARE If water is set to freeze, remove the pot and store it in a plastic bag in the basement until the spring thaw.

DISEASES/PESTS Remove diseased plants from water to avoid infestation. Spray off small pests with water.

OTHER SPECIES Momo botan, Perry's giant sunburst

POINT OF FACT Lotus flowers, seeds, leaves, and roots are all edible.

I GREW IT!

WHEN I GREW IT
DATE

NOTES

Broadleaf Arrowhead
(Sagittaria latifolia)

DESCRIPTION 2–4 foot (61–122 cm) tall and wide shallow water plants

HARDY ZONES 4-10

PLANT Plant tubers in soil at the edge of the pond or in a pot filled with garden soil and topped with gravel. Submerge so that the arrowheads are standing in 1–12 inches (2.5–30.5 cm) of water.

SPACE 4 feet (1 m)

CARE Trim stems after flowering to encourage new blooms.

DISEASES/PESTS Remove damaged part of plant if bacterial rot is showing.

OTHER SPECIES Appalachian arrowhead, Aztec arrowhead

POINT OF FACT Arrowhead tubers can be eaten roasted or boiled, hence its nickname "duck potato." Arrowhead is native to America.

I GREW IT!

WHEN I GREW IT
DATE

NOTES

....
....

PERENNIAL

Canna (Water Group)
(Canna)

DESCRIPTION A group of 2–8 foot (0.5 cm–2.5 m) tall flowers that grow in water

HARDY ZONES 7–10

PLANT Plant tubers in a pot filled with garden soil and topped with gravel. Submerge in water so that the base is 1–8 inches (2.5–20.5 cm) deep.

SPACE 3 feet (91 cm)

CARE In zones 6 and lower, pull the pot, store it in a plastic bag, and keep it in the basement over the winter.

DISEASES/PESTS Spray off small pests and remove diseased plants.

VARIETIES/CULTIVARS Endeavor, erubus, tanny

POINT OF FACT Tubers can be dug up and used again the next year in colder climates. Several cultivars were developed by crossing *Canna glauca* with terrestrial cultivars.

I GREW IT!

WHEN I GREW IT
DATE

NOTES

Water Lilies
(Nymphaea)

to

DESCRIPTION A genus of water plants with fragrant flowers growing on floating pads

HARDY ZONES Tropical: 10–11; Hardy: 4–11

PLANT Plant tubers (tropical) or rhizomes (hardy) in a pot filled with garden soil (not potting mix, because it will float away). Stems and leaves should remain unburied. Add gravel on top of the soil. Submerge the pot in water 12–18 inches (30.5–45.5 cm) deep. For tropical water lilies, the water temperature should be at least 70°F (21°C). Hardy water lilies can be planted after the last frost.

SPACE 1 foot (30.5 cm). They will spread naturally as well.

CARE Hardy water lilies can stay in the pond through the winter as long as the water doesn't freeze. If the water is set to freeze, or the lilies are tropical, remove the pot, place it in a plastic bag, and store it in the basement for the winter.

DISEASES/PESTS Spray off small pests. Remove lilies with fungal diseases.

VARIETIES/CULTIVARS Evelyn Randig, Wood's white knight, yellow dazzler

POINT OF FACT Water lilies help keep the pond clean. They cool the water, reducing algae growth, and their roots absorb chemicals from fish waste.

I GREW IT!

WHEN I GREW IT
DATE

NOTES

....
....

101 OUTDOOR SCHOOL
GARDENING ACHIEVEMENTS

1. Grow a plant in a pot.
2. Grow a plant from a seed.
3. Grow a plant from a seedling or cutting.
4. Measure sunlight to determine the ideal spot for a garden.
5. Plan a garden by choosing plants for your grow zone.
6. Prepare a raised or in-ground garden plot.
7. Select and use organic fertilizer.
8. Make your own compost.
9. Weed your garden by hand or with a hoe.
10. Grow a salad garden.
11. Grow a salsa garden.
12. Grow a tea garden.
13. Grow a butterfly garden.
14. Plant a fruit shrub or tree.
15. Plant a flower shrub or tree.
16. Grow berries.
17. Grow an avocado tree from the pit.
18. Grow a climbing plant.
19. Upcycle a container for plants.
20. Make your own potting mix.
21. Determine what kind of soil you have.
22. Measure the pH of your soil.
23. Amend your soil to better suit your plants.
24. Identify existing plants in your yard.
25. Identify and avoid poisonous weeds.
26. Grow chamomile.
27. Make fresh chamomile tea.
28. Grow mint from a cutting or seedling.
29. Grow a lemony herb.
30. Grow lavender.
31. Dry herbs.
32. Grow blackening herbs and spices.
33. Grow curry herbs and spices.
34. Grow fines herbes.
35. Grow Scarborough Fair herbs.
36. Make herbed root vegetables.
37. Grow a bay tree in a pot.
38. Grow a perennial herb garden year by year.
39. Grow catnip or cat grass.
40. Grow garlic from a clove.
41. Grow black pepper.
42. Grow ginger or turmeric.
43. Harvest seeds.

44 Plant lettuce from seed.

45 Try succession planting.

46 Grow greens.

47 Grow a cabbage.

48 Make a cabbage collar.

49 Grow rhubarb.

50 Grow asparagus.

51 Grow early potatoes.

52 Grow sweet potatoes.

53 Grow a tomato plant.

54 Grow tomato seedlings from seeds.

55 Grow an olive tree in a container.

56 Grow a pumpkin.

57 Grow a decorative gourd.

58 Harvest and eat squash blossoms.

59 Make a pole bean hideout.

60 Grow corn.

61 Plant a three sisters garden.

62 Add mulch to your garden.

63 Side dress a plant or tree.

64 Grow a unique vegetable.

65 Make homemade pesticide with water and dish soap.

66 Make a potato slug trap.

67 Grow strawberries.

68 Grow blueberries in a container.

69 Grow cape gooseberries.

70 Grow a grapevine.

71 Harvest nuts or berries.

72 Grow a watermelon.

73 Plant two apple trees that will cross-pollinate each other.

74 Plant a native pawpaw tree.

75 Plant any fruit tree.

76 Prune a tree.

77 Plant annual flowers in a pot.

78 Deadhead a flower.

79 Grow a sunflower.

80 Grow a perennial flower garden.

81 Plant bulbs.

82 Plant a flower shrub.

83 Plant a flower tree.

84 Grow a rose bush.

85 Grow a flower vine.

86 Plant a native shrub or tree.

87 Plant a succulent inside.

88 Propagate a succulent.

89 Plan a walled garden.

90 Plan a cottage garden.

91 Plan a homestead garden.

92 Grow a hedge.

93 Create a living pathway.

94 Create a water garden.

95 Make a natural living room.

96 Create a fairy garden.

97 Grow a sunflower fort.

98 Create a homestead garden.

99 Preserve fruit or vegetables.

100 Build a trellis.

101 Start plants indoors from seed and transplant in the spring.

INDEX

About the Creators

Bridget Heos is the author of the Kids' Book Choice Award–winning Mustache Baby series (illustrated by Joy Ang) and more than 100 fiction and nonfiction books for kids. Bridget lives in Kansas City with her family. She loves watching football, running and exercising, and exploring America via author visits to schools.
authorbridgetheos.com

John D. Dawson has created art spanning over four decades, from early years in advertising art to freelance work for the US Postal Service, National Park Service, United Nations, National Wildlife Federation, National Geographic Society, the Audubon Society, and the Golden Guide books. He and his wife, Kathleen, have lived on the Big Island of Hawaii since 1989.
jdawsonillustration.com